MOUSEHOLE

Coastguards & Wrecks

'BUTTS'

Mousehole – Coastguards & Wrecks

Cover Photograph: The netter, *Lady Catherine,* ashore at Carn Dhu, 13th December, 1983, she became a total loss (author's collection)

Cover Design: Tobi Carver

First Edition published 2013

Published by:
Palores Publications,
11a Penryn Street, Redruth, Kernow TR15 2SP, UK.

Designed & Printed by:
The St Ives Printing & Publishing Company,
High Street, St Ives, Cornwall TR26 1RS, UK.

ISBN 978-1-906845-48-3

MOUSEHOLE
Coastguards & Wrecks

'BUTTS'

PALORES

CONTENTS

H.M. COASTGUARD FORCE OF WIND TABLE

The Beaufort Scale with probable equivalents of the Numbers of the Scale.

Beaufort No.	Land miles per hour.	General Description of Wind.	For Coast use. Based on observations made at Scilly; Yarmouth and Holyhead.	For use of land based on observations made at Land Stations.
0	--	Calm.	Calm.	Calm, smoke rises vertically.
1	1-3	Light Air.	Fishing smack just has steerage way.	Direction of wind shown by smoke drift, but not by wind vanes.
2	4-7	Light Breeze.	Wind fills the sails of smacks, which then move at about 1-2 miles per hour.	Wind felt on face, leaves rustle; ordinary vane moved by wind.
3	8-12	Gentle Breeze.	Smacks begin to careen, and travel about 3-4 miles per hour.	Leaves and small twigs in constant motion; wind extends light flag.
4	13-18	Moderate Breeze.	Good working breeze; smacks carry all canvas with a good list.	Raises dust and loose paper; small branches are moved.
5	19-24	Fresh Breeze.	Smacks shorten sail.	Small trees in leaf begin to sway; crested wavelets form on inland waters.
6	25-31	Strong Breeze.	Smacks have double reef in mainsail. Care required when fishing.	Large branches in motion, whistling in telegraph wires; umbrellas used with difficulty.
7	32-38	Moderate Gale.	Smacks remain in harbour and those at sea lie to.	Whole trees in motion; inconvenience felt when walking against wind.
8	39-46	Fresh Gale.	All smacks make for harbour, if near.	Break twigs off trees; generally impedes progress.
9	47-54	Strong Gale.	———	Slight structural damage occurs (pots and slates are removed).
10	55-63	Whole Gale.	———	Seldom experienced inland; trees uprooted; considerable structural damage.
11	64-75	Storm.	———	Very rarely experienced; accompanied by widespread damage.
12	Above 75	Hurricane.	———	———

The fishing smack in the third column may be taken as representing a trawler of average type and trim. For larger or smaller boats and for special circumstances allowance must be made. This table should be posted up in each watch room.

Copy of a circa 1870 scale – author's collection

Penzer Point Lookout

I WAS ASKED by several people in our village to write down my experiences during my time as a Coastguard Watcher at Penzer Point as I'm the last one alive that worked there before it was pulled down. This is not quite true, there is one other person still alive who now lives in a secure home near St Ives. I regularly see his grown up children and always inquire how he is getting on. The lookout used to be a full time job but was downgraded to a 'bad weather watch' a few years after World War II finished.

I cannot remember the exact date but around 1963 I was asked by Ernie Hall if I would like to become a volunteer Auxiliary Coastguard watcher at Penzer Point Watchhouse. I readily agreed as this worked in very well with my fishing. I did two training sessions with Ernie who explained everything including how to keep the log book and the emergency numbers that might be needed. My Auxiliary Coastguard number was PZP 29, somewhere I still have my Coastguard badge with my number on it. They were very short of daylight watchers at that time, there was just Willie Cornish who was getting on a bit in years, Ernie Hall who was in charge, Cyril Torrie, Desmond Stone and Bob Smith were all working and did the evening and early shifts. We were only needed when the wind reached Force 6 or above and in foggy weather. The binoculars provided were basically useless, one lens would not line up with the other, they had been dropped several times over the years and were impossible to focus. After my first watch I went into Penzance and brought a brand new pair of 7 x 50 fully coated lens Swift Skipper binoculars which I still have and use today, 2013. If I remember correctly they cost around £18 to £20, and what a difference they made.

Penzer Point is the highest point between Mousehole and Lamorna with no house lights visible anywhere. It is about 2 miles from Mousehole and very remote. The only part of the watchhouse left now is its concrete base after it was decommissioned and pulled down in the 1990's. I was a Coastguard for 28 years at Penzer Point and received a long service medal after 25 years, if I had done another two years to make 30 then I would have had a bar for the medal but the watchhouse and LSA was closed down.

Looking back over those 28 years there are several things I should have done but didn't which I now regret. Why I didn't take a camera with me each time I do not know because the coastline really did change during my time as a watcher. The watchhouse view covered the whole of Mounts Bay from the Lizard Point to Porthcurno near Lands End to Gwavas Lake outside Newlyn. In those days this vast area of sea was a hive of activity with fishing boats, yachts, naval craft and dozens of stone boats calling into Newlyn to load crushed stone from Penlee Quarry for building roads. Every single craft had to be logged and put down in the large ledger. Anything unusual or in trouble had to be reported to Tol Pedn near Lands End, they were the main Coastguard station for this area at that time, now of course it is the Lizard Coastguard Station. Tol Pedn was closed down along with a lot of other stations but has now reopened with volunteer Coastguards manning the station. Once all the Mounts Bay stations were closed there was no lookout to monitor the Runnel Stone off Porthgwarra and nothing overlooking the Longships, both of which have claimed many vessels and seamen's lives over the years. Once Tol Pedn reopened that redressed the balance for these two areas. The government of the day said that because of all the electronic equipment used on boats Coastguard Stations were obsolete. Quite obviously these rules were made up by people who do not make their living at sea, there is still nothing to beat a pair of eyes looking out over the sea during dark stormy nights. Even today there are still fishing boats, yachts and cargo vessels lost every year at sea with no indication of that happening until the salt water activated distress signal is set off, by then the vessel in trouble has sunk. Water and boat's electronics do not go together and many lives have been saved by Coastguards seeing red smoke flares or distress rockets during daylight hours or at night.

Anyway back to the changing coastline near Penzer Point. There are numerous small and large caves between Mousehole and Lamorna all of which have local names. The Horse in the Stable is a narrow cave with a large rock inside it that looks like a horse looking over its shoulder. The white blaze of the horse's head is probably made by gull and jackdaw droppings and because it is well inside the cave does not wash off. I always threatened to paint a white tail on it but never got around to doing it, always too busy fishing or on watch. That cave cliff top has hardly changed unlike the Raven's Cave next to it. There used to be a stone hedge running along the cliff top to help protect the little meadows being worked by local men, there were also two large flat rocks jutting out of the cave cliff face where ravens used to nest. The ravens, their nesting place and part of the cliff top stone hedge disappeared during a southerly storm one night, as did the cliff top footpath to Lamorna. This cave has collapsed several times over the years and is still doing it today, it is now well over 100 yards from the stone hedge and cliff face. You can still see the stone hedge running towards the cave and carrying on the other side. Other parts of the cliff face have also been washed away but not so conspicuously as the Raven's Cave. A photograph taken when I started watchkeeping and one when I finished would have made good comparisons but unfortunately I didn't take any – a great pity. I wonder how many of today's young fishermen know the old names of various caves and rocks, they probably have their own names for them now.

I started off as a daylight watcher along with Willie Cornish but as all the other men were working ended up doing just as many night shifts. During one particularly bad southerly storm I did three six hour shifts in one day and regularly did two shifts per day. The shifts were from midnight to 0600, 0600 to 1200, 1200 to 1800 and 1800 to midnight, and when the clocks went back it was invariably me or Ernie Hall that had that watch giving a 7 hour watch. If we were on watch over the Christmas it was generally me or Ernie that did that watch, I had no family and Ernie was in charge and getting on in years so it didn't affect either of us very much.

A lot of strange things happened to me and some of the others over the years while on watch. There was one person who wouldn't open the door at midnight to anyone unless they stood in front of the window and he shone a light on you before letting you in. I don't know who he thought would be out there when it was pouring with rain and blowing a gale or worse, needless to say he didn't stay very long.

Back in the 1950's, 60's and 70's the horizon would be a mass of navigation lights passing up and down between Lands End and the Lizard, the vast majority of them small coasters. If you didn't know better the skyline looked like the coast with its twinkling lights. Penlee Quarry was working then crushing stone for road use and the small coasters loading stone in Newlyn carried on day and night, there were always two or three coasters waiting in Gwavas Lake just outside Newlyn for the pilots to bring them in after taking one out. In its heyday Penlee Quarry employed between 250 to 300 men and the quarry ended up 120 foot below sea level, there are plans to turn it into a marina and some work has already started. If it ever gets finished it could create 100 jobs with all ancillary businesses that are needed, shipwrights, sail makers, electronics as well as marina staff. I got very friendly with some of the coaster skippers that came into Newlyn for stone or stopped me out by the Wolf Rock Lighthouse for fresh fish. We always did a swap for fish – a basket of fish and they would load the basket with cigarettes and bottles of brandy. It didn't take the fishermen long to discover that the more stars around the bottles neck meant it was stronger and rougher than those with less stars. It never got thrown away and tasted quite reasonable if watered down with lemonade or tonic etc, if any was spilt when it was neat it invariably made the paint or varnish bubble up, I can't remember anyone drinking it neat. Most of these coasters were privately owned and from the continent, they nearly all carried their wives and children with them plus a teacher as part of the crew. They told me it was cheaper than buying a house plus they earned a good living, they all spoke very good English because they had to, English was and still is the international language for radio operators in all forms of transport – ships, planes and space craft. It also seems to apply to big international business now, especially the oil industry. When Penlee Quarry closed down this vast fleet of small inshore coasters dwindled rapidly. For some 60 years or more crushed blue elvin stone was used on roads, then they discovered it didn't wear out because it was too hard but just became smooth and slippery so they stopped using it on roads, seems a bit odd to me. An interesting fact that I learnt from Graham Robertson – he spent the best part of his working life at the quarry – was blue elvin is one of the hardest rocks and not even a thermal lance can melt it, the rock just glows white hot. A thermal lance melts granite which runs like water from the lance, I have seen this with my own eyes when they worked on the Longships Lighthouse and other granite structures. Graham told me that blue elvin was also used to line the outside of some bank vaults because it is so hard.

The busiest times at Penzer Point Watchhouse was always with a north or north east storm when all the small coasters travelling up the Bristol Channel or along the south coast would shelter in Mounts Bay. The most I can remember seeing from the watchhouse was sixty-four sheltering between St Michaels Mount and Newlyn and that did not include those inside Gwavas Lake that cannot be seen from the lookout. That was a Storm Force 9 north north east which lasted for three days during the late 1960's. During those three days our main job was keeping a close watch on the coasters, especially at night, because several started dragging their anchors. We would take a dead compass bearing and pass that on to Tol Pedn who would then radio through and warn vessels that were anchored that one or two vessels were dragging their anchors. We did not have a radio transmitter at Penzer Point and often had to use the aldis lamp so that vessels could check their bearings.

During another northerly storm in the late 1960's there were 43 coasters sheltering in the bay along with a submarine which turned out to be Russian. I passed this on to Tol Pedn who asked my to try and get the number or name. I couldn't see enough to do that but they must have passed that on to the Royal Navy because the next day two naval craft arrived and started searching the area on the bearings I had passed on to Tol Pedn. The submarine had left by then but the naval vessels spent all that day going up and down where she had been moored.

Another common sight was French or Belgian fishing vessels being towed into Newlyn during gales, either with engine trouble or their propeller bunged up with their fishing net. They tended to work much rougher weather than the smaller local trawlers. Really rough weather with high seas tends to stir up sediment or water in the fuel tanks which eventually got through to the injectors stopping the engine. Even with modern filters and traps this still happens today. I relieved Willie Cornish one lunchtime and he informed me that two Belgian trawlers, one towing the other, had rounded the Lizard and were heading for Newlyn harbour. Tol Pedn had informed him and it was logged, ten minutes later they phoned me up to keep a watch for these boats. It was a north west gale and the bay was white with broken waves, it was nearly an hour before I saw them and put the dead compass bearing on them. They were making very slow headway across the bay and when they got nearer I could see the wire trawl warps had two large tractor tyres fastened between them to act as a spring. These tyres were being stretched out straight during heavy surges as they slowly made their way across the bay to Newlyn harbour. When I was relieved and came off watch my replacement told me that most of our village was watching the trawlers progress across the bay through binoculars and couldn't believe tractor tyres could be stretched out straight.

A common practice in the 60's was throwing discarded trawl netting overboard which floated and was lethal to birds and boats. Small fish congregate under any floating material for protection, birds know this and inspect everything that floats. Gannets diving after fish get their heads stuck in the netting and always die unless released by kindly fishermen, the same happens to shags. Netting in a boat's propeller can and does stop the engine dead. This can cause a lot of damage and be very costly, especially if the prop or shaft gets damaged. Another strange thing that numerous fishermen have experienced over the years is that sometimes this man-made material will melt under water and run up the propeller shaft and into the boat before the engine stalls. This has happened to me once and was an expensive and time-consuming job to remove. First you have to disconnect the coupling, then draw out the shaft and propeller, then try and remove the melted material, once that is done remove all the stern packing and replace that. Most of this work could be done in one tide provided nothing went wrong. I managed to do mine with an hour to spare working from when the tide left the boat until she floated again. Others were not so lucky and as can be imagined a lot of swearing was going on. It must have cost the local boat insurance company a lot of money as they had to pay for the towage and any damage. It was the insurance companies and trawler owners that finally got the discarding of trawl netting stopped. Luckily no lives were put in danger but it would have only been a matter of time before someone was lost by being blown ashore.

It must be remembered that small VHF radios, which we all take for granted, were not available for fishing boats until about 1970 and they were all valve jobs. In any heavy weather when a boat slammed down off a wave it would quite often damage a valve resulting in the loss of radio communication.

One thing that fishermen and merchant men hate more than anything else is fog and in all probability more accidents and collisions at sea happen in fog than during gales. Once the visibility dropped below half a mile we were called out to be on watch. Nearly all the merchant men that go ashore in and around Mounts Bay do so in fog, why that should be is a bit of a mystery because they all have radar. Most of the Coastguards think it is because they set the radar alarms but fail to set them properly and leave it until the alarm goes off before checking. The number of times that forty or so small fishing boats working between the Runnel Stone and Wolf Rock have had to quickly get out of the way of coasters is staggering and when they pass you can see straight through the wheelhouse and there is nobody on watch.

Fog is a strange creature, sometimes it is patchy, other times as thick as a bag. It can be very low, a matter of a few feet, other times it goes from sea level right up high. One thing is for certain it certainly makes everyday things look totally different. Rocks and headlands you pass every day when fishing look strangely different and makes you wonder where you are, even though you know you still start doubting yourself when you can only see a few feet of rock.

Watchkeeping in fog was hard on your eyes – staring at a white blankness. Most of us relied on our ears. If it was warm you could lean on the railings outside or sit inside with the small side windows open. Sound travels really well in fog. If a vessel's engines sounded too close or you could hear voices on the deck we would fire off a flash and sound rocket to warn them off. We did have a fog horn but it was heavy and basically useless and locked away in a small cupboard. I can't remember it ever being used or leaving the cupboard – perhaps it didn't work. A loud hailer or megaphone would have helped but we didn't have one of those.

I remember relieving Cyril Torrie one morning, down in the village it was thick fog and you couldn't see the harbour quays when I left. Half way up Ragginis Hill you could see for miles, the fog was at sea level and only about 15 to 20 feet high. When I got to the Watchhouse Cyril told me you could see the boats' masts and hear voices but couldn't see the boats as they headed towards Newlyn for the early morning market. It was a strange sight and from what we could hear the fog was only from Penberth, Tol Pedn confirmed this when I phoned through to say I was on watch. At about ten o'clock I noticed a mast heading towards the shoreline very slowly, then a shout about rocks and voices enquiring about where they were. Cyril had already put together a flash and sound rocket ready for use before I relieved him. Taking that outside I put the stick in the pipe and fired the rocket, then I heard the boat's engines going hard astern and voices saying it was Penzer Point, after that they slowly made their way towards Newlyn.

The rockets had to be assembled before use, both the three star and flash and sound. There was a six foot stick with a notch near one end that the 15 inch rocket head had to clip into. That was then taken outside and placed in a firing pipe. On the bottom of the rocket there was a cone shaped wooden match, this was pulled off, then the paper from the rocket bottom was torn off. Holding the rocket head you scratched the cone shaped match across the rocket bottom and it fired immediately. There was no warning, it just took off. After firing one there were no hairs left on the back of your hand. A thick pair of leather gloves was provided but they were stiff and basically useless, they eventually disappeared, probably to be used as gardening gloves which was all they were good for. The rockets were rather lethal especially during a south east gale, then they would be blown around in the pipe and end up going inland.

I remember walking out towards the Watchhouse one morning to relieve Willie Cornish. I had already noticed the lights of a fishing boat very close inshore drifting towards the cliffs in a south east gale. Next thing a rocket went flying inland, not seaward to warn the boat. When I got to the Watchhouse it was about 0550 and Willie was putting together another rocket with great difficulty because he was shaking like the proverbial leaf in a storm. I gave him a hand and we had to jam the stick in with paper to stop it blowing around, this time it worked and the fishing boat moved offshore and headed towards Newlyn harbour. We could hear a lot of voices shouting and realised it was a French fishing boat. Tol Pedn was informed and they phoned back an hour later to say the French fishing boat was now safely moored up in Newlyn harbour. About halfway through my watch I heard the sound of fire engines out the back, switching the telephone alarm to outside I climbed up onto the top field and could see a lot of smoke and two fire engines slowly making their way across towards the smoke. I learnt later that a hayrick was on fire and was probably caused by the rocket that Willie let off that got blown inland.

Over the years several boats have run ashore between Mousehole and Lamorna. You can see the lights of both villages clearly when breasting the Lizard with just darkness between them and it is easy to assume that the coastline runs nearly straight between these lights but it doesn't. Lamorna Cove is set well back – if you draw a line between Mousehole and Lamorna the coastline between them is over half a mile further out, especially Penzer Point which juts out further than any other part of the coast.

The Watchhouse itself was a bit spartan in some respects, only a chemical toilet which nobody used. If you got taken short it was a bucket and chuck it job, if you wanted a pee you went outside and did that amongst the brambles and gorse, depending on which way the wind was blowing! We did have electricity and an electric kettle for making a hot drink. Heating was provided by a paraffin stove. During the night you drew a thick curtain across by the windows which stopped any reflection from the small dim light which was near the log book. There was a tall wooden backed stool by the windows in front of the dead compass and a small chair by the log book. There was also a very old battery-powered aldis lamp for signalling. The rocket heads were kept in a metal box and the long sticks in a bundle near the table. There was also a large wooden box of white smoke flares that we all used to rest our feet on when filling out the log book. These were eventually changed to red smoke flares. Just after that we were given hand-held flash and sound rockets to warn boats they were heading into danger and three star hand-held rockets to let vessels know we had seen their distress flares. I cannot remember any three star rockets ever being used except for practice purposes. I took the white smoke flares and used them for rabbiting when the wind was right. Light one and poke it down a rabbit hole, the wind would blow the smoke through the warren and rabbits would come out the other side coughing, sneezing and rubbing their eyes.

In the winter months during gales some fishermen would go lamping for rabbits most of the night. They often called into the Watchhouse to exchange a rabbit for hot cups of tea and a warm up. There used to be quite a few hares but for some reason they died out in the late 1970's early 1980's. Some nights when you were walking out through the lane towards the Watchhouse you would hear a thumping noise as hares ran down the lane towards you. If you stood perfectly still they would bump into your legs, hares cannot see in front of them and that is why they have to keep swinging their heads from side to side. The other animals you occasionally saw or heard were badgers crashing through the bushes when they heard you coming, there was and still are a lot of badger setts down towards the cliff bottom. I always took my dog with me and he was forever chasing foxes, he never got anywhere near one, same with the hares, but he used to come back into the Watchhouse with his tongue hanging out, bright eyed and tail wagging. He would have a drink of water then be off again.

I would quite often do the morning and afternoon watches straight off when no one else was available, 0600 to 1800 and those were the times that you saw some strange sights. Usually in foggy weather. One such day a middle aged man pushing a wheelchair with his wife in it stopped near the lookout. I asked him if he wanted a hand, he said no they were going to Lamorna on the cliff path. I looked at the wheelchair and told him that was impossible. He was not happy about that and basically told me to mind my own business. I did manage to stop him eventually and then I phoned up Tol Pedn and reported it. They got hold of the police who escorted both of them back to Mousehole. I very much doubted whether the wheelchair and his wife would have made it to Lamorna because there was a lot of climbing on the footpath in those days – the police agreed with me.

Another time during a double watch, in foggy weather in the summer, when I'd left in the morning it was just very thick fog, but once I was at the top of Ragginis Hill the fog got very wet, more like a fine drizzle which lasted all day. At 11.30 a very wet, cold, young lady walked into the lookout. She only had summer clothing on and it clung to her body like a second skin. I lit the paraffin stove and made her a cup of tea. She eventually told me that when she left Lamorna there was just a slight fog so she decided to walk to Mousehole along the cliff path. When she got up onto the high ground the fog got very wet and she gradually got colder. She knew about the Watchhouse and hoped someone would be there. She stayed about half an hour steaming in front of the stove as her clothes dried before thanking me and walking on into Mousehole.

Foggy weather during the summer months was always a busy time with visitors getting lost between Lamorna and Mousehole. A flustered or panicking parent would suddenly appear asking whether I had seen a young girl or boy walking towards Mousehole. Sometimes I had and other times I hadn't. When I hadn't I would inform Tol Pedn and they would call out the L.S.A., (Life Saving Apparatus) and police to search the cliff path and Lamorna. Those that did go missing were always found, some had to go to hospital but there were no fatalities.

Very occasionally the Watchhouse was manned during fine weather when a yacht that was making for Penzance was missing or overdue. I never did one of those shifts because I was always out fishing.

It must be remembered that during the 1960's there were no VHF radios or mobile phones and most ship to ship or ship to shore communications were with short wave or medium wave radio and routed through Lands End Radio Station. Several of us at Penzer Point brought a portable battery-operated radio known as 'Town and Country', I can't remember which company made it. By today's standards it was a large radio but it did pick up the shipping forecast, weather reports and the emergency channel so we could keep track of what was happening during emergencies. It had long, medium and short wave radio bands and being so high up at the lookout we could pull in radio stations that were impossible down in the village. During quiet nights I would slowly trawl through the short wave band picking up all sorts of strange stations, most of which I never stayed on. If you were lucky enough to pick up radio hams then that was always interesting.

A lot of the men that did the 1800 to midnight watch said they saw St Elmo's Fire dancing around on the flagpole and railings (static electricity). It always seemed to be that watch when it happened. In all my years up at the lookout I only saw it once and what an amazing sight. It suddenly appeared dancing around the flagpole and railings in a bright whitish light for about a minute or so then just as quickly disappeared to leave you blinking your eyes until they adjusted to the dark again. Another strange, unexplained thing that happened to some of the men was when they picked up the phone they got a slight electric shock. It never happened to me so I can't say what it felt like. The telephone engineers that regularly checked the wiring said it was caused by static electricity.

One thing that was a bit worrying was the large plate glass window that went across the front of the lookout. During severe south or south east storms it would bend inwards alarmingly, shooting water up the window as it compressed its rubber sealant. If there was a very large ground sea running during these storms then oarweed, small pebbles and winkles would be blown up the cliff to hit the window which always made you jump because it sounded like the glass was cracking. It never did crack because the rubber mounting just squeezed up taking the tension out of the glass, it always looked worse than it really was I suppose.

During daylight after such a storm you would quite often see a fox around the lookout picking up the winkles and eating them. Then he would work his way down from the Watchhouse through the brambles and gorse doing the same. I could never make out whether it chewed the shell to break it or swallowed them whole, anyway by the time it got down to the badger sett it shared with them the fox must have been very full of shells. They were a regular visitor to the Watchhouse because any stale bread was thrown out.

During the late 1960's at the height of the Cold War we did something called Atomic training which was rather laughable considering what we were supposed to do. According to the gentleman giving the lecture the main targets would be Goonhilly Satellite Station, Penzance Telephone Exchange and Cable and Wireless Station at Porthcurno. Penzance Telephone Exchange was the largest building in Penzance and handled all the foreign calls that were routed through to the Cable and Wireless Station at Porthcurno and then to every country in the world. The telephone exchange building is still there but now houses a large number of offices and art galleries. The Cable and Wireless Station is now a museum and well worth a visit. From what I understand the vast majority of the underwater cables are still in situ connecting most countries but not used. According to the museum all it needs is powering up to bring it back into working order. The cable to the Scilly Isles is being brought back to life to provide extra fast broadband for computers – they are hoping to have it working by 2014.

The Atomic Ministry man took out several strange objects from his case and proceeded to explain what they were for. The first was like a fountain pen, you twisted the top then held this up to the blast, this told you how big the bomb was by measuring the brightness of the flash and how high the mushroom shaped cloud was. Someone asked him how would we know when a bomb would be dropped? We would be informed when that was going to happen he said. He was also asked, if you know when they are going to drop the bomb why can't this plane be intercepted and shot down before it gets here? He didn't seem to have an answer to that and stood there looking at this pen thing, he eventually put that down and took out three other strange looking objects. He said they were for measuring radiation and various other things being emitted by the bomb. Then he passed around one small badge for us to look at which you pinned on your tunic. He explained that this told you how much radiation you were receiving. There were also several other things that you were supposed to do, after that pick up this red telephone, which was already installed in the lookout. This put you through to an underground atomic blast-proof station where you read off the readings on your instruments. The instructor did say that in all probability it would only be one bomb that would take out all three installations. I asked him how long we would live considering all three installations targeted were between 3 and 12 miles from our lookout. Until your badge goes red he informed us – probably 5 seconds or so from the initial blast. When I asked him how we were supposed to carry out all these tests and phone them through in 5 seconds he couldn't answer and just stood there blank faced. Well, I said, it will give us something to do before we turn into a melted glowing radiation blob on the floor. He didn't seem very happy with my reply and stood there scowling at me, perhaps being in the Ministry of whatever took his sense of humour away, if he had any to start with that is.

There was a lot of mumbling and grumbling from a couple of watchers and one of them stated that he was not going up the Watchhouse to die. I don't know how he thought it would be safer in our village than the lookout. If it ever did happen then the Lizard and Penwith peninsulas would basically be wiped out. Most of us just had a good laugh, we never did get issued with anything except the red telephone up at the lookout.

Daylight watches were my favourite because there was always something to look at. If there was no sea activity, there was always the wildlife that frequently came around the Watchhouse. I remember one time there had been a long hard frost and the ground was frozen hard. Woodcock and Snipe were dead or dying from lack of food and water. We all put out bowls of water for these birds and Cyril brought up a pick-axe and broke up some ground near the lookout for them. These normally very shy birds were scrabbling around near our feet to feed as the ground was broken, that's how hungry they were. The foxes and badgers ate all the dead birds and to them it was a banquet. We saw more dead birds during that spell than live ones.

At one stage the lookout at Penzer Point used to be manned full time, from what I can find out that ended just after the Second World War. The Coastguards Hotel, the little wooden L.S.A. hut, Coastguard Row and Parade Hill are all named after this service. Coastguard Row, just past the bus shelter, is a line of cottages on the left of a small road leading down towards the sea. This is where the Coastguards lived and in the early 1800's their lookout was the last building in this row. Parade Hill as you come into Mousehole is where the Coastguards used to parade for inspection. During the height of the smuggling period all the Mousehole Coastguards were arrested and jailed for turning a blind eye to the smugglers activities, as one reporter stated 'they did wear fog glass with banknote shades'. When the first Penzer Point lookout was built is unknown but probably in the 1800's. The modern lookout was pulled down in the 1990's. I cannot remember all the things that happened to me while on watch, all my personal diaries for that time were lost in a flood. Some things ended up good – others did not – with boats and lives being lost.

Southerly storm, May 1965. The fishing boat *Natasha* was wrecked in the harbour during this storm.

L.S.A. and C.R.E.

ONCE I BECAME a Coastguard at Penzer Point I automatically joined the L.S.A. (Life Saving Apparatus). I was also on the lifeboat at that time but only got called when the weather was really bad and I was not on watch. Jack Worth was coxswain and I did ask him once why he never called me when it was fine weather. "I can fill two lifeboats in fine weather but when there is a gale I want fishermen with me" was his reply. I was with Jack until he retired when most of the crew did the same. I learnt a lot during those eight years with Jack on the lifeboat.

Anyway the L.S.A. wooden hut where we kept our equipment was near the Coastguard Hotel at the top of Parade Hill. I have a photograph taken in 1870 when Mousehole Harbour was being extended that shows the L.S.A. hut in the same position and the same size. When we were closed down and disbanded in the late 1990's the hut was sold and became an estate agents office.

Mounts Bay has been a death trap for sailing ships caught between the headlands of Lizard Point and Lands End since records began. There is an oft quoted saying that for every foot of coastline in Mounts Bay there is a dead seaman and I can well believe that to be true after my research for my book *Mousehole – a documented history* which was published in February 2012. That goes into more detail regarding wrecks in and around Mounts Bay.

Back in the 1700's and 1800's there was a lot of outcry about the 'fearful loss of life around our coasts when boats go ashore'. It wasn't until the design of a rocket powerful enough to carry a thin rope a quarter of a mile to a stranded ship that lives began to be saved. Then the breeches buoy was invented to be pulled along the rocket line which changed the way hundreds of seamen were saved and rescue crews were formed all around the UK's coastline. They were all volunteers and known as the Rocket Crew. As equipment and rockets improved the name changed to Life Saving Apparatus, the L.S.A. Later still the name changed to Cliff Rescue Equipment, C.R.E., when helicopters carried out most of the ship rescues along with lifeboats. By then most of the work carried out by these coastguard volunteers was rescuing people who had fallen over cliffs or got trapped by rising tides. Once again the equipment had to be changed or altered to cope with different demands but we still kept the rocket and breeches buoy equipment. As the tourist trade increased so did the C.R.E.'s call outs. With modernisation Mousehole C.R.E. was closed down. There are now only two coastguard volunteer groups in our area and they are called Coastguard Mobiles, the nearest is Penzance Coastguard Mobile, the other is at Lands End.

Mousehole L.S.A. and C.R.E. did their training once every month or so with a regular Coastguard man, Don Buckfield. He was a good instructor and got decorated for bravery when we lost our lifeboat. Alan Johns was in charge and Cyril Torrie was our rocket man, I was the radio man. I can't remember the exact number of men but there must have been a dozen or more to shift all the equipment onto the lorry when we were called out. We all still referred to our group as the L.S.A. We eventually got issued with waterproof clothing with 'Coastguards' printed in white across the back of our jackets. This proved very useful with some of the more delicate jobs we had to do.

On Good Friday there used to be an annual pilgrimage with people walking through Mousehole to Lamorna along the coastal path, this had been going on for at least a hundred years. This particular Good Friday they were passing through Mousehole at 0700, it was a lovely day and by 1000 it was really hot. We were called out to help the police because there had been two rapes along the coast path, the police were in our village and Lamorna. Our job was to walk the path and ask anyone having sex if they were ok and did she agree to it. Needless to say some of the comments made by the men were rather blunt to say the least, but once we explained the reason they calmed down. Most of the ladies involved just smiled and said they were fine. When we got to Lamorna we went to the Wink Inn and had a few beers. Some of the people we saw on the coastal path asked if the rapist had been caught. The police did interview two men but I don't think anyone was actually charged.

I also volunteered my boat to do any coastal searches when needed. All I had to do was radio through to Falmouth Coastguards to say what and where I was and they would cover any damaged. I never did claim even though I hit the bottom several times. Thinking back the worst time was when six German students and their teacher got trapped by a rising tide. I was out on engine trials at the time. Anyway, Billy Kneebone was fishing in his boat which he moored to a crab pot buoy and jumped aboard me. There was quite a sea running and I slowly crept in towards the stranded people. Billy had the broom to keep the boat off the rocks, he asked them to come aboard one at a time, the first two did then the rest just jumped knocking Billy to the deck. The boat hit the rocks and nearly turned over before the propeller finally dragged us astern. I radioed through to Falmouth and let them know what had happened and that we were on our way back to Mousehole. Once there they all jumped out of the boat and raced up the granite steps without even saying thank you. I ran my boat up the beach and when the tide left her I had a good look underneath – just a long piece of wood gouged out of one bilge keel. That was in the 1980's and I expect that gouge is still in the bilge keel today, 2013 – the boat still works out of Mousehole, fishing.

Another time we had just got into Mousehole after fishing, Henry Hamblin worked with me then, when I noticed a lady running down the quay. She was perspiring and out of breath but she did gasp out that her young daughter was missing on the coastal path between Lamorna and Mousehole. We cast off and left the harbour. I radioed through to Falmouth that we would search the coastline and that the L.S.A. be called out to search inland. It was a slow search - 100 yards, then stop the boat and engine, shout and wait. No reply, then move on. This went on for nearly a mile until we were near the trees, this time we did get a shouted reply but couldn't see her. We told her to wave something above the gorse and brambles, eventually we saw a small white hand just clear of the undergrowth. I put Henry ashore and he slowly made his way towards the waving hand. I stayed in my boat to mark the spot for the L.S.A. They eventually got her onto the coastal path and finally into an ambulance that was waiting by the main road. By the time Henry got back I had moored the boat and washed her down and was leaning on the railings. He was laughing and shaking his head at the same time. "Poor little mite," he said, "she was only wearing a bikini type thing and she was cut to rags by the brambles, very frightened and distressed." Anyway the ambulance patched her up and gave her something to calm her nerves. The next day when we got in from sea the lady was waiting and gave a bottle of rum to each of us.

St Clements Isle just off Mousehole looks very close and a fairly easy swim. It is a lot further than people expect and is in fact a quarter of a mile from the gaps to the island. There is also a fairly strong tide running between island and shore, especially during spring tides. Most people tend to try and swim there and back with an overland north west wind when it looks calm. It is for a little way out, then the ripples start to build up into small waves near the island. Then it is difficult to swim back with the waves and wind in your face making breathing very hard without swallowing water. Every year someone, nearly always a visitor, gets stuck or in trouble when they reach the island.

I was coming in from sea one afternoon and noticed a lot of people shouting and pointing towards the island. Stopping the boat I listened to Dave Redhead who owned Mousehole News, a shop on the harbour front. He shouted down that some local lads had swum out to the island and were stuck. The lifeboat was out on practice and I called them up. Falmouth Coastguards answered and I told them what I knew. I couldn't get in really close because of the fresh north west wind which would have put me ashore as well. Next thing a Culdrose rescue helicopter arrived and lowered a man to the island. He eventually got the lads to swim out to my boat and I took them into Mousehole.

Another time a man had swum out to the island wearing a black neoprene swimming suit, he got there easily but couldn't get back. Every time he tried to get into the water he was attacked by a large seal which followed him from one end of the island to the other. There were several seal pups on the island at that time and Dave Redhead and myself were watching this through my binoculars. In the end I phoned up Falmouth Coastguards and they sent out the inshore lifeboat to rescue him. When the Coastguards phoned me back they were laughing. Seems our local amorous seal was trying to bite off his dangly bits when he tried getting into the water. They also informed me that there was no way he would swim back without being bitten, the seal was not at all frightened and even stayed hovering around the inshore boat. In all probability it had something to do with protecting their young seal pups.

Another time I was coming in from a day's fishing and noticed a white towel being waved. This was just past Mousehole Cave towards the lookout. It turned out to be two ladies in their twenties who had been nude sunbathing and were now cut off by the tide. I told them in another two hours they could walk back the way they came as the tide was dropping. They didn't want to wait so I picked them up and took them into Mousehole. Both ladies gave me a hand to land my fish by hooking the basket onto the line for me to pull up, then they both got into my van and helped unload and weigh my catch before putting them in the cold store. They told me it was a lovely warm, calm day and after climbing down into the cave proceeded along the rocks until they found a flat rock where they stripped off to sunbath.

There were a lot of instances where the L.S.A. were called out to rescue anglers trapped on rocks. Most times they were taken off by me and my boat. They waded across and fished quite happily until they noticed their rock had suddenly got a lot smaller. All they had to do was wait for the tide to drop then walk ashore, none of the rocks were ever covered in water except during gales. We often wondered if they thought the rocks moved up to match the tides and not get covered by the sea. There were and still will be a lot of fatalities around the Lands End area with anglers getting washed off low rocks. It usually happens on calm days when the sea is flat. Large ships passing along the horizon can and do cause a massive wake that can be up to eight feet high when it comes ashore. These large ships are invariably out of sight and passed by half an hour or so ago but the wake travelling at the same speed as the boat takes a lot longer to reach shore. One minute it is flat calm the next crashing waves that can sweep several feet inland catching unwary anglers and washing them off the rocks. This happens on a regular basis and even catches out local people, not always fatally but most times there is nobody about to raise the alarm or help you.

During busy summer months we would regularly be called out to look for missing swimmers between Penzance and St Michael's Mount. Someone would find a towel and clothing neatly piled up on a beach which had been there for hours, fearing the worst they would inform the Coastguards who would then call out Mousehole L.S.A. It would invariably turn out to be a false alarm with the gentleman forgetting exactly where he had left his clothes.

Mousehole L.S.A. covered a wide area from St Michael's Mount to St Loy Bay the other side of Lamorna and we had to attend any ship that went ashore. A French fishing boat went ashore in a dropping tide and fresh wind the other side of Penzance Harbour towards the Mount. She was in a sorry state when we got there and nearly on her beam ends. As the tide dropped she did end up on her side. Cyril managed to fire a rocket line across to the ship about 200 or 300 yards off shore, but the crew refused to haul the breeches buoy in. Their ship's dog jumped overboard and managed to swim ashore unharmed, one of the local people took the dog in. By now the fishing boat was starting to break up in the rough shallow water but eventually we managed to get all the crew ashore and taken to the Fisherman's Mission in Newlyn. Our L.S.A. crew got a certificate of merit award for that rescue.

We were usually the first on scene if it was at night or in a difficult place to get to. A mid water Grimsby trawler ran ashore one night just this side of Penzer Point lookout while she was processing the Mackerel she had just caught. We were the first land crew to reach her – the lifeboat and tug were already standing by. She could have been towed off easily because only her bulbous bow was stuck on the rock. I told the Mate that if she grounded she would be there for good because there were two large pointed rocks right underneath her midships. I had worked lobster pots all around that area so knew it well. Anyway the owners in Grimsby decided to leave her there – he had plenty of other boats like the *Conqueror* laid up. She eventually turned on her side and broke up, the smell of rotting Mackerel was overpowering for days. What is left of the *Conqueror* is now a popular diving site for visitors with plenty of conger, crabs, lobsters and other fish for them to see. I have a good set of photographs taken by me from when she first grounded to when she finally sank below the waves.

Then there was the twenty-eight foot *Lady Catherine* fishing boat that went ashore just this side of Lamorna in a southerly breeze. It was the only place along that stretch of coastline where you could walk off without getting your feet wet. We were the first on the scene and once again I have a set of photographs from when she first went ashore until she broke up and disappeared. With the southerly wind and swell the wooden boat did not take long to start breaking up. Before we left she had gone and the only thing left was freshly broken wood, nets and buoys strewn amongst the rocks. A great pity because she was a lovely looking boat.

Then of course there was the tragic loss of our lifeboat *Solomon Browne* and the coaster *Union Star* just the other side of Tater Dhu lighthouse. A full account of that night and following days is in my other book *Mousehole – a documented history*.

Another wreck that comes to mind was a Spanish coaster that went ashore in the early 1960's at Boscowen Point and basically sank within minutes. Three men managed to climb Boscowen and raise the alarm at a farmhouse. As far as I can remember they were the only survivors. How they managed to climb Boscowen Point in the dark and half a gale is a miracle – it is a hard enough climb in fine weather and sunshine. She was carrying a mixed cargo which included Spanish 12 bore shotguns, scent, bottles of whisky etc. The local divers had a field day during the next few weeks and our village was suddenly inundated with various types of scent, shotguns and bottles of whisky. Most of the whisky was ruined by salt water but a few did escape that. The scent was in small bottles and did not suffer from salt water. The Customs and Excise finally got the manifesto. The shotguns we had been using had not been nitro-proofed and were coming to this country to have that done. Most if not all of the shotguns were handed over to them before they blew up and killed the person firing them, the other stuff they did not worry about.

The last wreck near Mousehole happened on 30th November 2000 at 2300 hours. Mousehole L.S.A. had long been disbanded but we still all turned out. She was the Irish cable guard ship *Dolfyn*. She must have been travelling fast because she was halfway up the beach just past the North Quay car park. I could hear her propellers as she went hard astern from my house. Our lifeboat took the crew off because of a dropping tide, southerly wind and a large ground sea. By next morning she was already starting to break up and there was quite a gathering of people on the bank looking at the rapidly disintegrating ship with the words 'Guard Ship' in large white letters down her side. Edwin Madron looked at me and asked "What was the ship guarding? We don't have a cable under the village do we? Everyone laughed at that remark. Edwin is now our Harbourmaster. The Coastguard had men and a truck there every day and night for three days – mainly to stop people going aboard and stealing things or getting hurt. There were several instances of people getting their arms, hands or legs ripped open by the jagged metal. The worst to be affected were people's dogs. You would hear a yelp then a dog would go limping up the beach. They would get their paws jammed in v shaped jagged metal and panic. If they had just stayed still and let their owners pull their paws out the same way it went in it would not have been so bad. The worst I saw was an alsation which got its right paw jammed The owner ran down towards the dog that was desperately trying to pull its paw free but he was too late.

When the dog dragged its foot free there was no flesh, skin or pads left, just bone. He was carried up the beach and into the car presumably to a vets. I never saw the man again to find out how his dog was.

It was late summer 2001 before the wreck and beach were finally cleared of all metal. MOJO Marine did a fine job of the salvage work, cutting up the wreck and removing every piece of visible metal from the beach. I took a series of photographs from when she grounded until there was nothing left and the beach was cleared.

There were several other instances of fishing boats being lost out to sea within 2 or 3 miles of Mousehole, all of the men aboard were drowned. All of these plus others are in my other book Mousehole, a documented history, and go into more detail.

One thing Don Buckfield was keen on was training, he was the main full-time Coastguard for the Penzance area. Every six to eight weeks we had to do training in the evening during the summer months and it was always something different. St John Ambulance in Penzance taught us basic first aid and also mouth to mouth with the blow up doll called Resusci Anne. As you can imagine there were lots of ribald remarks from the men doing mouth to mouth with the doll, "don't fancy her", or "she's not very good as kissing", were some of the milder comments.

Most of our training involved the use of the line carrying rocket. Cyril and Alan were in charge of that. The rocket was a large heavy powerful one – it had to be so that it could travel a quarter of a mile in any type of weather dragging a light line behind it. It was made of metal as was the rocket launcher which stood on four adjustable legs and reminded me of mortars we used in the Army in 1956, rather lethal but saved countless lives around the UK's coastline. The heaviest piece of equipment was the large wooden box carrying the thick manilla rope that carried the breeches buoy across to the casualty once it had been pulled across and secured in place. There was also a large heavy double pulley block used for tightening the hawser before the breeches buoy could be used. Strange as it may seem one of the hardest things was finding a suitable piece of ground to bang in the opposing metal stakes. They had to be really secure otherwise they would move towards each other. When that happened the hawser would slide up the top stake and become slack. These stakes took all the strain from the hawser and the person being pulled across in the buoy, most times in mid air. All this equipment had to be loaded onto Alan's lorry, then unloaded and carried to where the casualty was, usually along cliff tops. You had to be fit and strong because sometimes this equipment had to be carried up to half a mile from the lorry, plus it was normally blowing a gale and pouring with rain.

I was the main radio and cliff top man If anyone had to go down the cliff face on a rope it was my job to be slowly lowered outwards until I could look down the cliff face and keep in radio contact with the people below. Basil Torrie was my anchor man and he always tied me on before letting me near the cliff edge. The first time was a bit scary but after that it was easy, each person had to trust the others when you were out on a call. I can't remember anyone getting really hurt, a few strains but that was all. The radios were large, heavy, cumbersome things with rechargeable batteries that only lasted about half an hour if you were lucky. I always took at least four spares with me when we were called out, two in each pocket. The batteries in those days were very heavy lead ones and measured some 6 inches long by 3 or 4 inches wide and 2 inches deep. Today the whole radio and battery is smaller and lighter than those old lead batteries. The only time I lost a battery was crawling underneath a tree that had blown down during the lifeboat and *Union Star* tragedy. Don Buckfield sent three of us along the Lamorna path to find exactly where the *Union Star* had gone ashore – Richard and Doug Hoare plus me. It was very stormy and wet and Doug gave up after a quarter of a mile. I radioed back for someone to pick him up which they did. That was the last time Doug came out with the L.S.A., he retired after that. Richard and myself carried on until we found the *Union Star*.

We did do our training in some unlikely places which Don Buckfield picked out for us. Penlee Quarry was one of them. It was still working in those days and their big yellow 25 ton trucks looked like Dinky toys from the cliff top. That was cliff rescue practice and we didn't need the rocket, just ropes, pulleys and stakes. Don nearly always went over the cliff with me lowered out to keep radio contact. He chose that place because it was a favourite spot for people committing suicide. We were called out there several times to look for bodies but they had usually sunk in the deep water that covered the quarry bottom because it was a hundred and twenty feet below sea level.

Another time we went to Lands End. We fired a rocket across an inlet and set up the breeches buoy. It was a bit nerve racking to be halfway across looking down three or four hundred feet to the rocks below at the tiny moving blobs that turned out to be large seals. It's surprising how carefully you examine the rope and pulley when you are slowly pulled across, one hair sticking out of the rope suddenly becomes a major flaw in your mind. Nothing really happened except your legs were turned into jelly by the time you got to the other side, but if your life depended on it you would quite happily be hauled to safety on a rope half that size.

We did use our rocket in some strange places but it was all good training. Another time we fired our rocket across Lamorna bay but that practice was cut short when the rocket landed amongst the heather and gorse and caught the opposite side of Lamorna on fire. We passed the fire engine on our way back to the L.S.A. hut. Needless to say we didn't do another practice at Lamorna.

We also did combined practices with our old lifeboat and Culdrose search and rescue helicopters. One helicopter practice at Lands End entailed being lifted up into the chopper from the ground. The down draught from the hovering helicopter was like being in a gale and you had to turn your face away to stop being blinded by dust, grass or small pebbles. Once you were right underneath the actual helicopter there was no down draught and you could work as normal. A lot of our practices were done at Lands End because it was so wild and rugged, especially during a strong blow but it was all good practice and stood the whole crew in good stead over the years.

The *Torrey Canyon*, aground on the Seven Stones Reef, 18th March 1967.

The *Torrey Canyon*, breaking up and leaking oil before she was bombed to try and burn the oil off.

The Rise and Fall of Fishing

MOUNTS BAY HAS a long history of fishing which dates back to the 11 and 1200's, before that time it was covered in a dense forest and a marshy bog. It was in 1099 that this vast area was flooded by the sea caused by melting ice caps and the land tilting back onto an even keel, this tilting is still going on today. The west coast of Britain has raised beaches and the east coast has sunken beaches. This tilting was caused by the vast, heavy ice cap that covered the continent during the last Ice Age. It was the monks of St Michaels Mount that recorded the flooding of Mounts Bay. 'There were forty villages and hamlets lost betwixt the Mount and Scilly Isles', 'all their crops, swine and beasts were lost and a great famine swept the land', 'the flood was so great that not even a man on horse-back could outrun it'. These are just a few facts recorded by them and all the above can be verified by the Royal Geological Society of Cornwall that used to be based in St Johns Hall, Penzance. My other book about Mousehole goes into more detail about that period of time.

It probably took several years before all the sediment settled and sea creatures gradually inhabited the seabed, fish on the other hand would take advantage of the readily available source of food from the churned up mud and be feeding on the outskirts of the muddy sea water. Certain areas of Mounts Bay are covered in thick Mud Stone which is riddled with Piddock shell holes. By the late 1100's there was a fishing industry catching Pilchards, Herring and to a lesser degree Mackerel. The limiting factor was a lack of salt for curing their catch. This lack of salt all changed in the early 1200's when King John 'granted licences to Bayonne salt merchants to fish for Whales, Conger and Hake from St Michael's Mount to Dartmouth'. From that time onwards the fishing industry began to prosper and expand, and as fishing boats got large they ventured further afield. By the 1500's great fleets of West Country luggers were sailing across to take part in the Newfoundland Grand Banks Cod fishery. On 20th July 1594 Sir Walter Raleigh and Sir Robert Cecil inaugurated and set in motion the first ever Naval Fishery Protection Patrol to protect the fishing fleet returning from Newfoundland loaded with Cod from pirates and Spanish men of war. This is probably the Navy's longest running patrol as it is still in force at the present time.

Up until the 1930's the biggest fishery was drift netting for Pilchards, Herring and Mackerel by luggers. At the height of the Pilchard drift netting in the 1800's there are reports in various newspapers regarding the numbers of vessels seen out in the bay. The numbers vary considerably from eighty to two hundred luggers, these vessels came from Mousehole, Porthleven and Penzance. Newlyn Harbour was not built until about 1900 although there were hundreds of fishing boats that gave their port as Newlyn at that period of time, their main harbour was Penzance. These very large landings of Pilchards from drift nets and seines were salted down for up to six months in very large vats. In Mousehole these vats were as large as a cottage living room and set underground.

Once the vat was 'broken open' the Pilchards would be arranged in a circle and pressed in a wooden Hogshead barrel, this removed the oil which was used in lamps and for cooking. The Hogsheads, weighing 50 stone, were for big buyers and suppliers, smaller two stone wooden boxes of pressed Pilchards went to smaller outlets and all were sent to Italy. This was still carried out by Nick Howell in Newlyn until the 1990's.

The Pilchard fishery nearly died out until the 1980's. Then when they were marketed under the name of Cornish Sardines and available tinned the industry picked up once again, now they are caught in ring nets during the winter months instead of drift nets.

The larger luggers would put Herring nets aboard and work all around the UK following the massive shoals. Some vessels went to Plymouth during the Herring season others to Ireland. From Ireland to the Isle of Man then on to Scotland and finally the North Sea. There are lots of instances when Herring boats would be away for three years before returning to Mousehole. With the advent of railways these very long trips enabled some of the crew to come home for a few weeks before rejoining their boats. There are numerous recorded incidents when men and boats were lost from both Mousehole and Newlyn in various ports around the UK during the Herring fishery in the 1800's. When steam drifters arrived the Herring were over-fished to such an extent that all Herring fishing was banned in the North Sea for a number of years to let the stocks replenish themselves. Now it is a tightly governed fishery with quotas and fishing is restricted to certain times of the year.

The other big fishery carried on from Newlyn during the winter months was drift fishing for Mackerel. There were only a few of the largest local boats that were employed in this fishery and from the records it appears that East Coast steam drifters came down to Newlyn for the winter months to take advantage of the vast shoals. They were larger and faster than the luggers that were slowly changing over to engine power. They could go out further and get back for the markets quicker. It appears from the records that huge shoals of Dogfish and Sharks were their main concern if they went off too far. If a shoal of Dogfish and Sharks found their nets full of fish they would soon reduce the nets to bare ropes. There are numerous recorded instances of this happening with steam drifters returning to the east coast with 'nothing but their bare ropes to show for their trip'.

Hand lining from small boats is the oldest known form of fishing and still carried on today. It wasn't until man-made fibre that didn't rot came into being that this fishery really took off. Jack Worth used to tell me about hand lining in the old days when we were out on the lifeboat, they all had a large wooden drier for drying natural fibre lines on and that they had to be washed in fresh water. From what he told me you had three or four lines drying and one each aboard the boat. In those days Mackerel were caught one at a time with a spinner. When man-made fibre became available along with strings of feathers then the hand lining really took off. When I started fishing Penberth and Mousehole had a dozen boats each, Lamorna seven and only a few from Newlyn. Once a good market was found and the price increased Newlyn soon had the largest fleet of small hand lining Mackerel boats. In those days there were just as many part-timers coming out after work to catch Mackerel as there were full-time fishermen – this kept the price of Mackerel low. Suttons was the main and biggest buyer for Mackerel in those days. Once the income tax people got hold of the part-timers then very few came out in the evening and it basically stopped. This increased the price for full-time fishermen and there ended up being two markets just for Mackerel – the early morning market and another around midday for the morning's catch.

There were two ways of fishing for Mackerel. There were the early morning boats that left around 0300 and fished for the midday market or the all day boats that landed in the evening for the first morning market. When the Mackerel moved offshore around the end of August beginning of September then two other hand line fisheries became available as other shoal fish moved in. Red Bream fishing was done with baited hooks between the Runnel Stone, Wolf Rock Lighthouse and Longships Lighthouse from August until November. The number of hooks used was around the fifteen mark, most used an old Mackerel trace but the hooks were rather small, we made up special lines for breaming and used a larger hook. These were baited with either strips of Mackerel or strips of Squid and you had three lines in the water at the same time as you drifted. Once you had fish on one line you waited until another line had fish on then you could carry that shoal with you for a long time. In my own view this was the most enjoyable fishery of the lot but alas did not last long as will be explained later. It was also a very lucrative fishery with Bream fetching a good price during those months. On a good day it was possible to catch 60 stone of

Bream. At seven shillings and sixpence a stone in the late 60's it was always a good Christmas boost. A stone is 14 pound in weight.

Another good fishery that sadly did not last long was catching Spur Dogfish, known throughout the Second World War as Rock Salmon. This again was mainly a winter fishery when the large shoals came in to breed over rough rocky ground. There were several ways of catching Dogfish, baited hooks similar to Bream but with much bigger hooks. A bottom line of 1,000 hooks baited with Mackerel or a rope that went round the boat with hooks every eight feet on strops with leads next to the strop. This was pulled in on the working side, fish taken off and baited then the line slid over the opposite side to form a loop under the boat some twenty feet down. As long as you kept pulling this line in it very seldom tangled but it was hard work.

Once the big shoals of winter Mackerel were found offshore in the late 1960's this changed the inshore Mackerel fishery completely. Long liners, inshore trawlers, crabbers, netters and Mackerel boats that struggled to make a good living during the winter months were now all employed on the winter Mackerel fishery. This proved to be a very lucrative fishery in what was normally the hardest time of the year.

These massive shoals started off in Mounts Bay and then moved round the Lizard into Falmouth Bay where they spent most of the winter months. At the height of this fishery the *Western Morning News* estimated there were one thousand five hundred boats working out of Falmouth which was the main base for this large fleet. Some smaller boats only had a crew of two, the majority had three or four men with the largest boats up to eight crew members. If you take an average of three men per boat that makes four thousand five hundred men, and for every two men aboard a boat there was one man ashore sorting, packing and transporting these fish. That is according to the newspapers, not my figures. These vessels came from all along the south and west coasts to take part in this bonanza. The Mackerel were all large prime fish that had come in to spawn and mate and in March they dispersed into small shoals and probably moved off to deeper water because after that date the huge shoals seemed to disappear. It worked out that each man caught on average between sixty and eighty stone of Mackerel a day.

We had about 7 years of very good fishing from Falmouth during the winter months then they let in the big industrial mid water trawlers and ring netters from around the country and continent. Three years later this fishery was dead – overfished – and it has never recovered, even after 35 years. Some Scottish vessels found the Red Bream fishery and they killed that in one year. This fishery has never recovered either and now if one of the hand liners catches a Red Bream it normally makes local news amongst the inshore boats. If both of these winter fisheries had been left to the hand liners then it would still have been going today. Some of the Scottish skippers and crew we met told us several times "if you don't stop us we will kill this fishery and put you all out of business." They were honest enough to tell us that and what they caught each trip. They also knew how much the whole fleet of hand liners caught in a week and calmly told us that they caught more in one night than all the hand liners put together did in a week. They told us it couldn't last and it didn't. Marine scientists tell us that it will never come back to what it used to be with the massive shoals of Mackerel that used to stretch for miles.

There were large industrial processing vessels from Japan, Russia and other countries that made the *Scillonian* look like a small trawler when she passed them. These processing vessels had hundreds of people working in shifts 24 hours a day, especially the ones from Japan.

That last season we left Mousehole and steamed around to Falmouth in August/September. We worked our way up as far as Plymouth and back again, finally arriving in Newlyn just before Christmas. None of the boats caught enough Mackerel to land – that was the end of the winter Mackerel fishery. I took photographs from the top of the old ice works showing some 1,200 Mackerel boats moored up in Newlyn that winter. Exactly how many people were put out of work is unknown but some reports say as many as eight thousand in Cornwall and Devon lost their jobs when that fishery collapsed. This figure seems rather high to me but the inshore fishery from Mousehole, Newlyn and Penberth really nose-dived during the next two years with very few vessels working. It was especially noticeable from Mousehole as nearly all the boats have to pass our village on their way to sea.

I sold my big boat and had an eighteen foot Plymouth Pilot fibreglass boat built in Penryn. Those fishermen that carried on turned to tangle netting for Crawfish, Monkfish, Ray and hopefully Turbot. As the Crawfish gradually got overfished and Monkfish prices increased we relied on Monkfish to make up the difference. In those days you had to cut off the head which was about half their size and weight, my best catch was just under 20 stone of Monkfish tails and a box of Brill in one day. I gradually turned over to gill netting when monofilament nets became available, this proved much more profitable with Pollack, Hake, Dogfish and Wrasse making up most of the catch. I was the first boat to do this and what surprised me most was it took two years before other boats turned over to gill netting. Once that happened the huge shoals of Dogfish that used to come into the bay to give pups were soon depleted, now there are basically no Dogfish in the bay.

It became harder for small boats to make a living and a lot of them changed over to working crab and lobster pots, others just left the industry to work ashore. I had a basket of one thousand two hundred hooks that I used to bait up with Mackerel and shoot occasionally for Conger, Ling, Ray and Turbot when the weather and tides were right. The wildly fluctuating price of Conger sometimes made this unprofitable.

The price of Blue Shark was high so a lot of boats turned over to catching them for a few years. Now it is illegal to land any type of shark because they are classed as endangered.

One hand line fishery that has survived and still provides a good living for single handed boats is Bass fishing. When I first started in the 1960's you had to make your own lures from surgical rubber tubing or red rubber cycle inner tubes. The hooks you brought in packets of one hundred, they were bent so that the lure would spin when being towed. We used two large bamboo poles that were used in the carpet trade to hold a roll of carpet, you had to drill small holes in each section to stop them splitting in hot weather when the air expanded. A block of wood was drilled with two holes to take the pole ends, this was screwed onto a thwart or engine box top. A rope leading from where the poles went over the gunnels up to the bow stopped them sliding backwards, one rope for each pole. A piece of car inner tube on the end of each pole acted as a spring to take the strain when a fish took the lure. Most of us also had another line over the stern with a heavier weight on so that they would not tangle. It did not take companies long to produce lures suitable for this type of fishing that could be used both commercially and by anglers. I found the best to be West Enders which were made on the Lizard by a small home based company. The supply of large thick bamboos suddenly increased with most fishery suppliers stocking them. This fishery now gives some boats a very good living from mid summer onwards. These hand line caught Bass now have a tag clipped into their gill covers to say who, where and when they were caught and always command a higher price as it is classed as a sustainable fishery. If I remember correctly this was started in Newlyn by the local Bass fishing boats. Live baiting with small Mackerel is used quite a lot in this fishery but catching Mackerel small enough is becoming more difficult each year. I had a small Sprat net which I used to catch Sprat to use as dead bait. This was a brilliant bait provided that the Sprat was very fresh, everyone would catch a fish but not always Bass. Pollack, Coalfish and especially big Wrasse would take this bait before a Bass had time to find it, again it was a very hit and miss bait because you could not depend on catching any Sprat.

Hand lining for Squid still goes on but that is a very short season lasting only a month or so when they come close inshore to breed before dying. Some years there are plenty, other times very few, so not something you can rely on, but the price was always very high for fresh caught Squid.

When I think back to when I first started fishing so much has changed over the years. The way we now fish with modern fishing gear that doesn't rot and the electronic equipment that finds fish for you. When I started my research for my Mousehole book in 1963 there were still a few old fishermen left in their late 80's and early 90's that started their fishing careers under sail in luggers. They had rhyming sayings for everything to do with fishing all of which I wrote down but unfortunately they along with some of my early diaries where lost when my house was flooded. It is easier to remember rhyming sayings than those that don't. Those relating to fishing still apply to this day.

> Gulls a sitting on the sea there'll be plenty of fish for you and me.
> Gannets circling overhead there'll be fish enough to go with the bread.

If you didn't feel like going to sea that day then this saying or excuse helped.

> If the candle blows out its too windy for a shout,
> If it stays alight the sails can't take flight,
> So its back to the missus for the rest of the night,
> In the lee of bum island you snuggle up tight.

The old men seemed to have one-liners for nearly everything in those days, nearly all about boats or the weather. 'Dark as a dogs guts' relating to weather, 'Porthleven built' meaning the vessel had a wide stern, now used by some of us to describe ladies with large posteriors, 'Rough as a sack full of nails', used for vessels that were not properly looked after, as was the saying 'As ugly as a bag full of assholes'.

Before echo sounders came in fishermen had to be very observant and watch out for what sea birds were doing. If you saw several Greater Black-Backed Gulls sitting quietly on the surface then you knew that underneath them was a shoal of fish. They were waiting for bigger fish like Pollack or Bass to drive them to the surface. Likewise Gannets or Herring Gulls circling high in the air meant there was a shoal of fish underneath them that were too deep for even Gannets to attack, they were patiently waiting for the shoal to be driven to the surface. Sand Eels are the main food for most fish and if you saw these rashing on the surface you knew there were Mackerel of other fish chasing them. There are two sorts of Sand Eeels, the Greater and Lesser, and it is the Lesser Sand Eel that everything tries to eat, even the Greater Sand Eel. Upon the arrival of the first Lesser Sand Eels in Mousehole gaps we would take our tangle nets out into the bay and shoot them across Perran and Praa Sands for Ray and Brill.

We found this out by accident in the late 1960's and it still held good, although the number of fish caught was declining, until I packed up fishing in 1999. It lasted for about a fortnight, when the Sand Eels first came ashore early in the year, then the fish moved offshore.

Tides and knowledge played a big part in catching fish in those early years, most of that I learnt from the older fishermen. All of which still holds good to this day. If you wanted low water slack at the Runnel Stone then you waited until the flood tide had reached the plat on the New Quay steps, by the time you had reached the Runnel Stone every float and bobber would be idly floating on the surface. The tide does not suddenly rush in everywhere but has to move from one part of the country to another and the first of any flood on the Lands End Peninsula creeps along the shore and then slowly moves outwards into the bay. Some of the old fishermen could tell the time by just looking at streaming dahn markers. I couldn't but I did know when I could just creep into Mousehole Harbour on an ebb tide before the boat grounded by how much of certain rocks were above water. I never knew the names of every rock between here and Lands End but all the lugger skippers did. I think Jack Worth made a tape of the names used by the lugger skippers for every point and rock between Newlyn and Lands End.

Unusual Sightings

BACK IN THE 1960's two fishermen rounded the Lizard on their way to Newlyn to land the catch of Pollack that they had caught hand lining over wrecks. There is a long line of Second World War wrecks stretching from near the Eddystone Lighthouse to the Longships and Scilly Isles known by the local fishermen as Bomb Alley. These were all merchant ships sunk by German submarines which would hide in the deep gullies and were basically undetectable until they ventured out to attack a convoy. One submarine made a bad mistake and was chased from the Wolf Rock Lighthouse right around Mounts Bay before being sunk by Naval escort vessels near the Lizard. Wolf Rock Lighthouse was a favourite hiding place for submarines but in the deep gullies around the lighthouse they had to be careful because the strong tides could sweep them onto the rocks. Imagine the surprise when fishing boats, going out for a day's fishing, found a German submarine stranded high and dry on the Wolf Rocks. The German crew were rescued and interred for the rest of the War. The submarine eventually sank into one of the deep gullies where it remains to this day and is home to countless fish, not really fishable with nets because it is so close to the Rock itself. Night-time fishing in Mounts Bay was banned by the Government for the duration of the War because they were often attacked and sunk. The local newspapers have some very good photographs showing the submarine high and dry balancing on top of the rocks.

Anyway, back to our two fishermen coming in to land their day's catch. They were off the Lizard still gutting fish followed by hundreds of Herring Gulls when they saw what they described as a large headed sea serpent. There were no radios in those days so it wasn't until they had landed that they told anyone. You could not find two more level-headed fishermen who hardly ever smiled or cracked jokes but you can imagine the leg pulling they endured for the next few months. Both men were adamant that they had seen a monster but regretted telling anyone. It did get reported in the local papers and for the next twelve months there were numerous reports of people seeing this sea monster around the Lizard and Falmouth Bay areas, all of which were reported to the papers and local television stations. All the modern fishing boats have sonar and fish-finders pinging away so any self-respecting sea monster would keep away and try to find somewhere quieter.

It was usually in the autumn when the Gulf Stream was close inshore that you saw strange things. Modern fish-finders have a temperature gauge set in the transducer so it is easy to find the Gulf Stream because the temperature jumps up from about 8 or 10 degrees in the colder inshore water to around 15 to 18 degrees when you hit this warm current. This warm water basically runs passed the Longships and inside the Wolf Rock lighthouses, that is the nearest it comes to the shore but with a south west wind some very strange things get blown into the bay. Portuguese Man-of-War jellyfish and the purple By-the-Wind Sailor both have little gas filled balloons which keeps them on the surface and so are easily blown by the wind. Very occasionally you would see large shoals of white Swimming Crabs with their large flattened legs just under the surface. They never leave the Gulf Stream, keeping to the warm water current unlike the local Swimming Crabs that spend most of their time on the bottom.

Large shoals of Bass and Mackerel in the Gulf Stream attracted Whales, Dolphin, Tuna, and Swordfish and these in turn brought in the Killer Whales and big Sharks. Before the Mackerel were over-fished Pilot Whales were commonly seen and the occasional Great White Shark. Porbeagle and Blue Shark were quite common and on sunny days Hammerhead Shark were sometimes seen at Mullion or Porthcurno swimming over the sand. During practice flights Culdrose helicopters normally saw them over the sand and if people were swimming they would use their loud hailer to warn them. It was always reported on the local news and local papers. Very occasionally a Hammerhead would get caught up in tangle nets and be landed at Newlyn.

Mid water trawlers fishing for Mackerel or Bass would sometimes catch Tuna but that was not a common occurrence. One mid water trawler landed a huge catch of Bass at Newlyn and several of us weighed the largest of those we could see before they were sold. The biggest we found weighed 49 pounds and the vast majority had deformed mouths or hooks still in their jaws from beach anglers. All the hooks we saw were far too small and the line that was still attached was way too light to handle a big Bass. The rod-caught record is around 20 pounds but a lot of Bass landed that day were well over that weight.

Leatherback Turtles were often seen and if a really large one was on the surface in calm weather its neck and head could be three or four feet above the surface which often gave rise to sea monsters when seen from the shore. The biggest I ever saw was about ten feet long. I don't think anyone believed me until the *Scillonian* reported seeing one that was about twelve feet long while on her way to the Scilly Isles that morning. They regularly see Leatherback Turtles between Lands End and the Scillies and now have a wildlife volunteer aboard to tell visitors about what type of bird, dolphin, whale or turtle they are looking at. Several fishing boats reported seeing an Albatross but it wasn't until the *Scillonian* reported seeing one that it made the national news. They eventually found that it spent a lot of time during the breeding season, along with other nesting seabirds, on a small Scottish island and has been photographed by experts several times. They cannot explain how it crossed the equator but think it must have landed on a ship that took it into the northern hemisphere. I saw it once out by the Wolf – it must have had a wing span of about ten feet and made the Gannets look very small. Whether it is still alive I don't know but what a sad, lonely life it must have led being the only one of its species this side of the equator.

Another time when we were steaming off what we thought was a large turtle head sticking out of the water proved to be a very large mahogany tree trunk sitting upright in the sea. When we got closer you could see that the bottom of this log was a mass of Goose Barnacles. There must have been a ton or more to upend this massive tree trunk which looked like it had been in the sea a long time. Another boat decided to see if there were any fish sheltering under the barnacles, there was and he caught twenty-five stone of Wreckfish which he landed at Newlyn. After that most boats checked out any floating wreckage but that was the only large landing of Wreckfish. We often saw them when we were drifting during shark fishing trips, but only single fish. Guy Duder caught a nice Wreckfish aboard my boat on one trip that turned out to be the junior rod-caught record for this fish. We had to go to Plymouth Marine Aquarium to get it verified and as far as I know is still a junior record. He and his brother Garth are now both grown up and have families of their own. Their father Vyn had the fish stuffed and mounted in a glass case which I presume they still have – I must ask them next time they are down.

Over the years trawlers have dragged up a variety of strange things. Trevelyn Richards was the skipper on one of Stevenson's trawlers and lived in our village and some of the things he told us were quite amazing. On one trip they trawled up a complete dead elephant – where it came from was anyone's guess – it probably died on board a ship that was transporting it and thrown overboard. Another time it was an Airforce flying boat that had the bones of the pilot still inside – a Second World War victim. Unexploded bombs were regularly trawled up or caught in tangle nets. I caught one small bomb in tangle nets and when it got to the surface I just cut the netting and let it sink back to the bottom. The young lad with me went right up the bow. I laughed and said "If it blows up being up there won't make much difference!" Normally boats that trawl up a bomb are kept outside the harbour until the Bomb Squad arrives to blow it up. Not always though. On one occasion when we came into Newlyn to land our fish, there moored against the quay was a trawler with a bomb merrily swinging from the mizzen mast boom. The Bomb Squad eventually took it out to Low Lee and blew it up. I doubt if any of them would blow up even if you hit them with a sledge hammer after 30 years or so under water, not that I would like to try belting one with anything. There was one report of a torpedo being trawled up but I don't know where or when this happened. I don't think it was Newlyn but can't be certain.

There are so many funny things and tragic accidents that happened during my fishing career that it is difficult to remember all the names and boat skippers involved. Those that entailed me are easy to remember but there weren't many of those, mostly other boats that were in the right place at the right time.

There was one fisherman who could not swim and was frightened of drowning. Every time he went to sea he tied himself to his boat with a rope. Another fishing boat coming in from sea, I think it was Sam Lambourne's vessel, noticed a boat off Lamorna with nobody on board. He jumped aboard the drifting boat and found it was empty. When he pulled in a rope there was the body of this fisherman who used to tie himself to the boat. He had drowned but how he came to be overboard was never established. She was towed into Newlyn and the police took over.

Another time a boat was found going round in circles whiffing for Mackerel off St Loy. Once again there was no one on board and no body was ever recovered. This also happened to a Mousehole boat. The Mousehole boats had been fishing for Red Bream near the Wolf when the wind freshened from the south east and we all decided to pack up. I was the slowest boat in those days and Billy Worth said he would wait for me by the Runnel Stone. When I passed him he waved me on and said he would catch me up – she was the fastest of the Mousehole boats then. I got to Mousehole and moored up – still no sign of Billy. An hour later Jack Worth knocked on my door and asked me if I had seen Billy. I told him he was at the Runnel Stone. The lifeboat searched all night along with other Mousehole boats. It was the next morning that his boat was found adrift several miles off the Longships by a Belgian trawler. Engines working, fishing lines still in the water but no Billy – his body was never recovered either. This sort of tragedy happened to quite a few single-handed Mackerel and crabbing boats over the years around the Lizard and Lands End peninsulas. In most cases no body was ever recovered.

During the winter Mackerel fishery in Falmouth all of the Newlyn boats that fished for Suttons landed their catch at the Custom House Quay. Everyone was in a hurry to land their catch, clean their boat and pack up. There was not a lot of room for landing if all of the boats came in at the same time, you just had to wait your turn. There were numerous fights over landing spaces and especially boxes. The Suttons drivers would reverse down the quay loaded with fish boxes but they nearly always stayed in their cab until all of the boxes had been either kicked or taken off and the fighting had stopped. Every day there was an argument over boxes which often led to a fight which the drivers kept well clear of. It seemed a bit pointless as there were always plenty of boxes to go around.

The Custom House Quay Harbourmaster wore a dark blue uniform full of gold coloured braid and a peaked cap with gold coloured braid and the word Harbourmaster on it. He was a very short man that didn't come up to my shoulders and very officious shouting at skippers during landing times. He did have a difficult job during the winter months but that did not excuse the way he talked to some fishermen. This particular day he must have been in a really bad mood and just shouted at everyone. He was definitely not liked by the fishermen. Saturday afternoon after landing I was in the Chain Locker pub talking to Clive Hosking about the fishing. The Harbourmaster pushed between the two of us to get a drink. He always had to buy his own, no fisherman ever got him a drink. Anyway Clive was well over six feet and a big man – I just about came up to his shoulders. When the Harbourmaster pushed between us we both looked down. Clive was smiling and had a twinkle in his eye. We pretended he wasn't there. "What do you think of the Harbourmaster here?" asked Clive. "Not a lot," I said, "he acts like a little Hitler and wouldn't last a day in Newlyn." He was looking up at both of us but we just gazed over his head. "What are you going to do if he speaks to you like that again?" Clive was having a job not to laugh. "Throw the little bastard into the harbour," I said. By this time we were both having a job not to laugh. The Harbourmaster took his beer and melted into the crowded bar. Several other fishermen said that if I didn't do that they would. All the boats were fed up with him and the way he treated most of us.

The following week when we were coming up to Custom House Quay to land James Howard from Sennen waved me down. "You don't have to throw the Harbourmaster in the harbour because I've done that and been kicked out of Falmouth." From what I was told he was doing his normal shouting and James picked him up and threw him into the middle of the harbour. Another boat used his gaff to drag him aboard. Everyone was asking if they had managed to stick the gaff in him, but they hadn't. When we got in to land his hat was still floating in the harbour. I can't remember whether that was rescued or left to sink. The following day he was really nice to everyone and was like that until the fishery collapsed a few years later.

A lot of boats had to moor up at the Prince of Wales Pier further up the river because there was no room at the Custom House Quay. One boat found an old long line hook, fastened twine to it and baited up with half a Mackerel before leaving. The next morning when he pulled it in there was a fine seven pound Bass on the end. From then on most boats did the same. If it wasn't a Bass it would be a big Thornback Ray. It was illegal to shoot nets in the estuary which was a pity because it was full of big Thornbacks, anglers catch some really good sized ray in that estuary.

When the oyster dredgers were working in the estuary it was like going back a hundred years. All these old boats were only permitted to use sail power – no engines were allowed on board. It truly was and is a spectacular sight to see them all under sail in a stiff breeze towing their oyster dredges which they then have to haul in by hand. This is one of the oldest and most controlled fisheries in the country and for that reason will carry on forever with no over-fishing with those involved making a good living. If nothing else it shows that conservation does work.

The south coast of England from the Isle of Wight to Lands End has some horrendous tide races that are so strong that a small boat cannot forge ahead if they are battling against it. Around the Isle of Wight the Lanby Buoys marking the passage have a large saucer-shaped bottom that helps to keep them on the surface. Other places do not have any buoys, just lighthouses. Portland tide race off the Bill is very difficult – you either have to go round two hours before high water and keep within a few yards of the headland or go several miles offshore. I remember once not keeping in close enough and suddenly found my boat going backwards even with the ninety horse-powered engine going flat out. Once she was angled back towards the shore we got round easily.

When coming back from Falmouth you always picked an ebb tide, this would sweep your boat past the Manacles, Black Head, round the Lizard and carry you halfway across the bay. The waves off the Lizard tended to be very short and steep in a big spring tide on the ebb. We came round one winter in such conditions, Bobby Carswell was with me that winter. I noticed several coasters had stopped and turned in towards us so I told Bobby that someone was in trouble and to keep a good lookout. As it happened the Lizard Coastguards had seen us and another fishing boat and thought we were in trouble which we were not.

Another time we came round the Lizard in a snow storm with plenty of Mackerel on board to land at Newlyn. We were on our way back from Falmouth after a winters fishing there. If I remember right Paul Gilchrist was with me that winter, I do remember having to throw water over the cabin window to clear the snow a couple of times. Anyway we got into Newlyn just as Suttons was packing up and managed to catch their last lorry. I told them another four boats were following me all full of large Mackerel.

Once you round the Lizard and see the old lifeboat slipway going straight up and down you wind the wheel around until you are heading north west. Keep her on that course and you will run Mousehole Island down. Likewise south east if you are making for the Lizard from Mousehole.

The Longships inner tide is a bit strange with eight hours ebb and four hours flood so a lot of water has to flow past the Longships during a flood tide, but the flood was always good for hand lining when after Pollack. The shallow ground off Hella Point, just inside the Runnel Stone, was well named because during a flood tide the seas build up into very short, steep-sided waves which was a hell of a point to round when going to the Longships.

The Buck Rocks off Tater Dhu Lighthouse had an odd tide as well. If you were working nets or pots a quarter of a mile off you would have ebb tide until those two rocks were covered by water, then flood tide until they were once again well clear of the sea and sticking up in the air. There are of course several other places inshore that do this. In the middle of Mounts Bay the tide slowly turns clockwise in a big circle, always a good place to anchor and fish with baited rods or hand lines when you could find a big area of very rough ground. We usually anchored up on 'the Drop Off' or 'Hump' once we had found the edge. From my research this was once the old beach before the bay was flooded back in 1099 – it basically runs from off Lamorna right across the bay towards Kynance Cove where the Serpentine rock is quarried to make colourful ornaments. Serpentine quarrying is now strictly controlled and as far as I know the only other place it is found happens to be in South Africa.

Back in the mid 1960's I met a university student who was panning for gold where the stream comes out in Mousehole by the Monument. When he left Mousehole he went to Lamorna stream to do the same. He told me he was working his way through college by panning for gold in various streams and rivers in Cornwall. It must have paid because this was his third year of doing it. I saw him a month or so later and was surprised to see his jam jar with a quarter inch or so of gold dust in it. He seemed pleased with the results so far and was off towards the Lands Ends area to carry on panning. I don't know how much Cornish gold fetched in those days but he assured me it was worth doing. I never saw him again to find out how well he did but if it got him through college it must have paid off.

Stream and sewer under the 'Lobster Pot Hotel,' emptying into the harbour, 1960 (above). The same view, July 2012 (below).

A Changing Harbour

BACK IN THE 1800's Mousehole was probably the busiest fishing harbour in Mounts Bay. There were so many fishing boats using our harbour that they had to land their catch end on over the bow – there was just not enough quay space to land side on. The harbour in those days was constantly being cleared of rocks, stones and sand that built up each year. This was well documented in the Harbour Commissioners' Minutes Book from 1869 when the New Quay was being built. This was kindly lent to me when I was doing research for my book *Mousehole – a documented history*.

By 1900 Newlyn Harbour was up and running and the vast majority of the Mousehole vessels had moved there. It had everything our harbour didn't. Plenty of space – forty acres inside the harbour where most vessels were afloat at any stage of the tide and a rapidly expanding market for fish-buyers. Mousehole Harbour Commissioners now advertised for part-time Harbourmasters that could top up their wages by fishing – this still applies to this day. Prior to that all Harbourmasters were employed full-time.

When I first started fishing in about 1962 Clarry Williams was the Harbourmaster and some of the old rules still applied. No boat was allowed to moor against the quays unless they were full-time fishermen – when he retired this rule was slowly relaxed. Now there are more part-time fishing boats and pleasure boats moored on the quays than full-time fishermen but there are also far less vessels fishing for a living. Back then there were about fifteen small full-time boats working from Mousehole, mainly hand lining for Mackerel, and three crabbers. At one stage it dropped down to just two boats, myself on the New Quay and Phil and Frank Wallis on the Old Quay. That lasted for two years until Tommy Rowe built his own boat and started full-time fishing after leaving college. There are now about six full-time and four part-time boats working through the summer months (2012) mainly hand lining and crabbing.

Back in the 1960's there used to be a large pit of water some two or three feet deep inside the harbour mouth at low water, the paving in the harbour gaps would be clear of water. I can remember youngsters like Chris Cass and Francis Harris wading around in the pit catching fish, mostly Flounders – the Mullet tended to be too fast for them. In those days the last tier of boats on the New Quay would be afloat before they could leave the harbour, we had to wait until the paving was well covered. Especially the older deep-drafted boats like *Porth Ennis*, *Onward*, *Quo Vadis* and *Merlin*.

The newer boats, *Internos* and *Harvester*, had less draft and were usually the first to move. This pit has long since gone filled in with sand brought in for the visitors.

There used to be rungs let into the quay from the plat leading down to the harbour bottom from the steps on the New Quay, now you can't even see this plat anymore. Running around the harbour top a line of granite mooring posts, which the main heavy harbour chain runs behind, used to be a good four feet up in the air, now they are buried or just visible above the sand. After the installation of the first sewerage system the square manhole cover near the slipway was six feet above the ground, now it is nearly covered with sand. I don't know how many thousands of tons have been dumped in our harbour over the years but it must be quite considerable. Some areas of our harbour are now four feet shallower than they were in the 1960's, mainly from the New Quay steps that used to have four rungs leading down to the harbour bottom upwards, on the Old Quay it is roughly the same. During big ground seas a lot of the sand gets washed out of the harbour and there are now some large areas of sand between the Island and shore.

There used to be three very heavy chains running around the harbour for boats to put fixed moorings onto. I know the gaps and top harbour chains are still in situ but I'm not certain whether the middle chain has been renewed for the running moorings. If it hasn't then it must be getting very worn and thin. A lot of pleasure boat owners tend to put down their own weights to fix the bottom running moorings onto. Sand is very abrasive and soon frays rope and wears away the little spindles on pulleys if you are regularly using your running mooring, three years is about their lifetime. We found the best thing instead of a pulley was those large red-brown insulation blocks used by electricity companies, they don't block up with weed etc as quickly but sand will eventually cut a grove into even these. If there is a big ground sea with a lot of surge in the gaps before the sand has had time to be compacted it is quite usual to see sandy coloured water swirling around halfway to the Island. The incoming surge or run sweeping into and around the harbour stirs the sand up and the out-going surge or run carries it out between the Island and shore. During very large ground seas you can see boats moored in the harbour straining sideways on their mooring ropes as it sweeps around the harbour. This is the time that some boats break adrift due to weak moorings, normally they part out their stern lines which take the most strain and are nearer the gaps, very few part out bow lines. Little damage is done because the loose rope invariably gets tangled in other moorings preventing any damage by being swept ashore. I can only ever remember one punt being swept out of the harbour and that was saved by Jimmy Madron and Clive Hosking back in the late 1960's.

There are times when other punts are taken out with the ebb tide in fine weather but that is mainly because they were tied up with a 'slippery hitch', at least one a year is seen floating around the harbour. Another rare happening is when someone moors their punt up too tight against the quay, their boat usually ends up in mid air. I've only seen this once and this particular time it was only about two feet from the harbour bottom, but I have been told of punts that were six feet above the bottom.

When electric bilge pumps first became available they caused a lot of problems. You had to switch them on and off manually. If you forgot to turn them off they would empty the boat of water – with no water to keep them cool they got very hot and eventually burned out the small motor. To my knowledge no vessel ever caught fire which is surprising having seen the melted remains of some pumps. Now all modern electric bilge pumps are fitted with float switches that you switch on and forget about.

A natural follow-on from electric bilge pumps were electric deck washers and they were dangerous. They always had a long pipe so that every part of the vessel could be washed down. After use the pipe would be hung overboard and the pump switched off. In a lot of cases the water in the pipe ran back into the bilge causing a suction from the sea that filled boats up and sank them if it was unnoticed. The only fishing boat I know that actually sank at sea was coming back from the Longships after pulling tangle net gear. I think she was named *Scath Ross* but I'm not certain. She had been using her deck wash and hung the pipe over the side. She sank off the 'House and the Hole' the other side of Tater Dhu Lighthouse in the late 1960's, all the crew were saved. They did eventually raise the boat and bring her into Newlyn for the Marine Investigation people to inspect – they were the people who said it was the deck wash back suction that caused the accident. Now most deck washers are fitted with a one-way valve to stop this happening.

All fishermen are supposed to wear life jackets but try doing a day's work aboard a boat wearing one and it soon becomes clear that it makes your job twice as hard. They tend to be bulky and restrict your movements. The first type of life jackets were lethal, not only were they very bulky but they had so many places that nets could get caught in that it was much safer not to wear one. The next type out didn't have so many buckles etc on them but they were still unsafe to work a long day in. They are constantly improving the design of life jackets to make them easier to work in but what the latest modern ones are like I can't really say – I stopped fishing in 1999.

The vast majority of larger fishing vessels use calor gas for cooking. If the calor gas bottle is not on deck and leaks, or the cooker is not well maintained and gas leaks it becomes very dangerous. Calor gas is heavy and will always sink to its lowest level which in a boat is the bilge. If the leak goes undetected the gas level in the bilge becomes a bomb waiting for a spark to ignite it. Once that happens the gas explodes and it rips the vessel apart without any chance of calling for help. There are so many boats lost in this way and its not until the Marine Accident people get involved that they discover what had caused the loss of the yacht or fishing boat. Gas alarms are now fitted to try and prevent these sorts of accidents but they still happen occasionally.

Unlike a car, if anything goes wrong when you are at sea you are stuck with it, you cannot get out and walk away. Fishing is the most dangerous job and every year in the Mounts Bay area there are fishermen that put to sea and never come home again. Whether you go to sea for pleasure or to earn a living the only thing between you and possibly death is the thickness of your vessel's hull. All life originated in the open sea and she is generally known as the 'Cradle of life', but sometimes this cradle turns into a grave.

Mousehole Harbour is evolving and changing to meet different demands now that there is more space compared with the 1800's when the harbour was full of luggers. To survive as a paying concern it has to. Car parking on the quays is the main money earner for the harbour these days. Then mooring fees from the local and visiting craft. Mousehole is still classed as a White Fish Port and they are trying to get more fishing boats to land here during the summer months when the harbour is open. According to the Harbourmaster the Commissioners are thinking of installing a small cold store and small electric hauler for pulling boxes and baskets of fish up the quay sides. The very end of the New Quay is reserved for fishermen's vans.

During the Christmas period the harbour is full of floating electrical decorations such as serpents, whales and yachts. Every road and street has strings of electric bulbs and in the surrounding hills there are large displays lit up. This brings in thousands of people who all spend money in the various shops, eating and drinking houses in our village. On November 5th and New Year's Eve Chris Cass puts on a magnificent firework display with money donated throughout the year by locals and visitors.

Once a year our rowing club holds a regatta with boats from all of the rowing clubs in Cornwall and Devon taking part. Every three years there is the 'Sea, Salts and Sail' which draws old luggers and sailing craft into our harbour. Some of these old sailing craft not only come from the UK but from the Continent as well with France and Breton being very well represented. The number of canoes and skiffs increases each year and not only from locals. Visitors also bring them down strapped to car roofs. All these things help to make a colourful and well used harbour.

Broken baulks after storm, 18th December, 1983.

The author's boat – *Butts*, 1980.

The author shooting gill nets from *Butts*, 1980.

This shot produced just under 20 stone of Monkfish tails and three stone of Brill, October 1985.

The mackerel boat *Golden Corn* ashore at Mousehole, late 1960s.

The Grimsby registered mid-water trawler *Conqueror* ashore near Penzer Point, 28th December 1977. She had been trawling for mackerel and was declared a total loss.

Southerly storm force 10, wave breaking over quay heads, 18th December, 1983.

Rescued and smashed up punts after a southerly storm, 2002.

On December 19th 1981, sixteen people lost their lives from onboard Penlee's lifeboat *Solomon Browne* and the Irish coaster *Union Star* after she ran aground near Tater Dhu lighthouse (pictured). There were no survivors from either vessel. The *Solomon Browne*'s engine and deck plates, plus other metal, were found alongside the rock below the lighthouse by local divers Bob and Hazel Carswell. There was a large patch of blue paint and missing barnacles on this rock as well.

Pictured some of the wreckage of the *Solomon Browne* the following morning in Lamorna Cove.

The *Union Star* wrecked near Tater Dhu. The ship's skipper, his wife and two daughters and four other crew members lost their lives.

Mousehole CRE crew and volunteers forking back seaweed in the search for bodies, 21st December, 1981.

The Scottish mid-water trawler *Bountious,* which sank three miles off Mousehole Island with no survivors. She had been trawling for mackerel and was brought into Newlyn after being raised on 4th January, 1980.

The trawler *New Pioneer*, ashore near Penberth, 1988.

The Irish Cable Guard ship *Dolfyn* went ashore 2300 hours on 30th November 2000 by Bank Car Park, Mousehole. The Penlee lifeboat took off all the crew. The next morning, 1st December, the *Dolfyn* was completely covered.

The *Dolfyn* breaking up fast. She was deemed a total loss and MOJO Marine finally cleared the last of her the following summer, 2001.

Bad Weather

MOST BAD WEATHER is predictable and the Shipping Forecast that is broadcast every three hours informs you in advance of what is expected. Before VHF marine band radios became available in the late 1960's early 70's we relied on our barographs or barometers. I have both and over the years they have proved themselves to be indispensable. There is also a very old barometer set in the wall near the Ship Inn for the benefit of fishermen. In the early years not all bad weather was predicted though and it did catch several vessels unawares.

I can remember going to sea in the mid 1960's in the biggest ground sea I have ever seen. Even the old fishermen were saying the same. Jack Worth said he had never seen a sea like that even when he was on the lifeboat. There was a lot of run in the harbour and we all had difficulty in getting out. It was a case of waiting your chance for an outer surf then the outside boat of the tier would go. There were seven boats and we all waited until the last boat, Jack Worth's *Porth Ennis*, was out of the gaps before heading westward. There was not a breath of wind and there hadn't been for weeks but the ground sea was massive. The Island was nothing but white water going right across it. It was this big ground sea that washed away the last of the few scraggly bushes and brambles whose seeds were carried there by gulls building their nests, this still happens but now only grass or weeds. The trough between the waves was roughly two lengths of *Porth Ennis*, she was the largest boat at 26 feet, and she had to climb over the waves. It was a strange sensation to find your boat going uphill on a green wall of water. There were no breaking crests just huge rounded waves that rolled slowly into the bay. Every single piece of shallow ground was breaking white and the Runnel Stone was just a boiling mass of white water. The Penberth boys said they had never seen anything like that before because some of the rocks were briefly out of the water. Just off Carn Dhu Luther Pender's boat, *Lyonesse*, turned around and headed back to Mousehole. It wasn't until we got back after fishing that we found out why. He was closer inshore than most of us and a huge wave broke over the bow and smashed in the forward cuddy breaking every piece of glass. Ned Tregenza was with Luther then and both men had to go to hospital for serious facial cuts. Ned was very lucky not to lose his right eye. By midday these huge ground seas had gone and it was not until the evening that the local television station mentioned that the large seas rolling in along the south west coast were caused by a hurricane off America. Jack Worth and David Sleeman both reckoned they were about twenty feet high. In forty odd years fishing I have never seen anything that big in calm weather. The aftermath of hurricanes in America often effect the south west but it depends how far north they are, the further north the more likely it is to effect the south west coastline.

Another time during a very big ground sea there were seven of us waiting outside the gaps to come in. You have to pick your time exactly during these conditions because it is easy to lose control as the surf is so strong. You try and pick the time between the outer surf and inner surf when there is less movement. *Porth Ennis* was always the first in because she was the biggest, once moored up the next boat would go until all were safely moored. I was nearly always last as the *Merlin* was only 19 feet long. When I came in there was a bit of a panic going on because Dave and Eddy Sleeman's boat, *Internos,* was right up under the Lobster Pot Hotel and had been swept there by an inner surf and left high and dry. The inner surf had spun Billy Worth's boat, *Onward*, around and she was sticking stern out making it impossible for *Internos* to moor up. Once I was moored we eventually got a rope across to *Internos* and we all pulled her across during the next inner surf to moor up outside of me.

Another time the *Girl Barbara*, which was being worked by Vic Cowan Dickie, was spun around in the gaps by an outer surf breaking her mizzen mast boom. Luckily there were enough fishermen down on the quay to get a rope onto her and pull her into the harbour before the inner surf took control. Nearly all the boats that work out of Mousehole now are eighteen foot fibreglass vessels that are much lighter than the old wooden boats.

The only wind that can build up waves big enough to cause any damage to Mousehole Harbour is from the south because this wind has a thousand miles of open ocean to blow across before it reaches land. The Lizard Peninsula and Mousehole Island protect the harbour from a south east wind, and the land between Mousehole and Lamorna protects the harbour from a south west wind. All the big storms that cause damage come from the south, the Ash Wednesday Storm on 27th February 1963 that caused so much damage to the coastline in Mounts Bay was from the south. Mousehole, Newlyn and especially Penzance were all badly damaged during that blow. Lands End Coastguard Station and Culdrose Airbase on the Lizard recorded winds of 130 miles per hour. This was a Force 12 on the Beaufort Wind Scale which is classed as a hurricane. There was a lot of ground lost to the sea that day. Penzance seafront lost the most and it changed the area around Wherrytown for ever. Penzance Promenade was smashed up as were all the seafront properties. Newlyn was not much better while Mousehole had its quays badly damaged and all the baulks smashed. There has only been one worse recorded storm in this area and that was on 7th October 1880, that caused even more damage and there were some two hundred fishing boats smashed up. My other book *Mousehole, a documented history* gives more details on these two storms and the damage they caused.

There is another strange phenomenon that only appears to happen on calm hot days when the wind suddenly flies from the north east and when it does it really blows, building up a very short sea with breaking wave tops. It seems to happen around midday and dies away in the evening. From what I can find out it has something to do with temperatures which causes air on the land to suddenly rush out to sea. Hot air normally rises but this appears to be in reverse with hot land air rushing towards the sea. I asked Plymouth Marine Laboratories for an explanation and the answer they gave me was that the sea was hotter than the land but I have never known our seas to be 20 degrees centigrade.

I have experienced this several times during my forty years of fishing. The first time was back in the 1960's when we were fishing all day for Mackerel at Porthcurno Sands. One minute it was calm and the next there was a frizzer howling out of the Bay. David Sleeman came alongside me and said "Don't worry boy, get inside the headland to fish, this wind will die away come evening." We all moved in closer out of the worst and carried on fishing. By evening when we were steaming back it was once again flat calm.

Another time I was out by the Wolf working gill nets, I think it was Henry Hamblin with me then. It was a calm, very hot day and it felt like the sky was sitting on your shoulders. Henry was saying it was damn hot and hoped it would soon cool. I had looked back into the bay several times because I thought the wind might fly. This time when I looked back there was a line going across the dark water racing towards us out of the bay. "Don't worry Henry," I said, "it will soon be very chilly." We got the last tier in before the wind hit us and Henry said "Where the hell did that wind come from?" We slowly made our way in to Lands End out of the wind and shot away the last tier we had pulled around Nanjizel Bay. We did some hand lining until the evening when the wind had dropped. Another time I was actually working lines at Lands End trying to catch Turbot when the wind flew. Again I had to wait until evening before going home.

Nobody deliberately goes out fishing in bad weather but occasionally you do get caught out especially in fog. How many times that has happened to me I can't remember as it was quite a common occurrence. Before Decca, and later GPS, became available all the boats used to know the compass bearings to certain points and how long it took. All you had to do was trust yourself and in thick fog that can be difficult believe me. I knew the exact course and time from the Wolf to the Runnel Stone Buoy but when you can't see anything you do begin to doubt yourself, especially when you think you should see what you are aiming for. Did I allow enough on the compass or watch for the way the tide was running, that was the usual thing going through your mind. I remember coming back one time in very thick fog. I can't remember who was with me but every so often he would nearly disappear in the fog. We had been working a piece of ground about six miles south east of the Runnel Stone. When we packed up I set a course for Mousehole and kept an eye on the watch and echo sounder. My watch told me we were nearly there and the sounder was shoaling up fast, so I eased the throttle right back. I stopped the boat but we couldn't see or hear anything so I stopped the engine. Then we heard people talking, dogs barking, cars and a bus but still couldn't see anything. Starting the engine I slowly eased her forward until the bow man shouted he could see something. I walked forward and we both looked up at people's faces peering at us over the end of Mousehole quay. After mooring up we landed our catch at Newlyn. That was the thickest fog I can remember being out in.

Another time we left Mousehole in a fog when you couldn't see the Island. That was aboard the *Streaker* – a twenty-one footer. Andy and Miff Wheeler were aboard, they were not keen on going out. They thought it was a waste of time. I told them if I could find the first tier we would find all our nets. I had timed the distance and course between each tier of nets and the course and time to Shag Rock on the Island. We had tiers of tangle nets from three or four miles back of the Island right across the bay. After 45 minutes I asked Miff to stand on the side decking and look out for our dahn flag. We basically ran that down. After that we worked our way right across the bay going from one tier to the next without missing one. It was evening before we got back in and it proved to be a good day's fishing.

When Decca first came out it proved to be very susceptible to certain types of weather conditions which could and did affect the radio beacon transmissions. These beacons were placed around the UK and Ireland and sent out radio signals which were picked up by the Decca and gave you your position. But as everyone knows radio signals can be affected by certain weather conditions. Remember the odd breaks in television transmissions years ago? Well Decca was even worse. It could jump lines or sectors or even blank right out. Thunder and lightening was the worst but heavy rain or fog did affect it as well. Some fishermen had got to rely on their Decca to such an extent that they didn't know what course to steer if it went down in fog. Several times in those early years of Decca you would hear a boat asking another what course to steer to reach Newlyn. I often wonder if any of today's young fishermen bother to write down the course and time it takes to get to certain places – like the Runnel Stone to the Wolf for instance or when to change course to follow the coastline back to Newlyn or Mousehole. Now they rely on GPS to get them back in foggy weather, but what would they do if the GPS went down or they lost their electrics?

Fishermen do tend to rely on electronic equipment too much because it is easier and I have to admit that I did once. Mathew Wheeler and myself were bringing a boat back from Fowey to Mousehole that we had just bought. She was a 28 foot Cygnus fibreglass vessel named *Miranda*. What we didn't realise until we left was that she didn't have a compass light but there was electronic self-steering. It was 0100 when we cleared the estuary and rather foggy. Using a cigarette lighter I set the self-steering on the compass course to take us to the Lizard. Half an hour later we passed a coaster anchored up with a small rowing boat and two men inspecting the coaster's rudder area. Half an hour or so later we passed the same coaster again! I slowed the boat down and disconnected the self-steering. We both thought the self-steering was working harder than it should and finally found that the belt was too slack to work the wheel. Not having enough light to do anything about it or to see the compass made it very difficult and the thick weather did not help either. It was a matter of checking the compass every twenty minutes with the cigarette lighter. Just on daylight we picked up the Manacles Buoy, after that I opened up the throttle and it was an easy and uneventful journey back to Mousehole. Once back the first thing I did was install a compass light. After that incident the first thing I did when delivering a boat was to check for a compass light and I also carried a good torch. The furthest delivery I made was from Weymouth to Mousehole but that was my own boat – most deliveries were from Falmouth to Mousehole or Newlyn.

After fog the worst sort of weather was snow. This always built up on the glass wheelhouse windows making it impossible to see out of. Car windscreen wipers were no good because the salt ended up scratching the glass giving it a foggy appearance. Larger trawlers have a small, round, thin, fast-spinning piece of glass that throws water and snow clear which used to be called 'Clear View'. Smaller boats resort to throwing a bucket of water over the windows.

When I first started fishing the majority of small inshore boats were completely open to whatever the weather threw at them. We had all been fishing at Porthcurno for Mackerel and on the way back a heavy hail storm started. I could not see where I was going and ended up holding a wooden box in front of my face and looking through the little slit in the bottom until it had passed. This caused a lot of laughter with the bigger boats. Once we had landed I went into the loft and made a small aft wheelhouse that looked like a pill box because it was straight. I put in one forward and two side windows, it was just tall enough for me to stand inside. It took me two afternoons and evenings to make then fix in place aboard the *Merlin*. I had to do this with two other vessels I bought over the years - *Carn Dhu* and the *Butts* - all my other boats had forward dodgers. Once radios became available and later fish-finders these stern wheelhouses became invaluable - they also help to keep you warm and the flying spray off your body. If you are coming home or going out in driving rain, snow or hail it is virtually impossible to keep your head up all the time, it's a matter of trying to peer under the hat brim or a quick glance up every so often. Now of course all the small boats working out of Mousehole and Newlyn that are out every day fishing have either a forward dodger or a small stern wheelhouse. Out of the two sorts of dodgers I preferred the stern wheelhouse because it left the bow clear and gave you more room when working nets or lines, and if you wanted to anchor up you didn't have to clamber around a forward dodger to tie your anchor rope. One of the most useful things aboard a boat if you were working any type of fishing gear or anchored up was a mizzen. Once set the mizzen would keep you on the nets, pots or lines you happened to be working, especially in any wind. It was like having another man aboard steering the boat. If you were anchored over a wreck or high rock then it would keep your boat pointing into the wind instead of yawing from side to side. It was also brilliant for keeping you over a shoal of Mackerel with the engine ticking over just fast enough to keep you in one place or slowly going ahead. When I was working lines and nets the first thing I did before leaving the harbour was hoist up the mizzen sail. The simple act of having a mizzen set made working anything so much easier. The local sail maker always made my sails and I always had them in black material. You hardly ever see a fishing boat with a mizzen these days - I think the modern day haulers are so powerful that they have basically made mizzens redundant. There is one thing a hauler cannot do and that is to keep your vessel facing into the wind if you are anchored and they cannot help steer your boat in a fresh breeze - both of which a mizzen can do. Back in the 1960's when there were a lot of long liners working out of Newlyn they all had mizzens. They might be working up to one hundred miles offshore and if the wind was set fair then several of them would hoist up foresails to help out the engine and save fuel when coming back to port. The last vessel I can remember with the foresail up was the *Renovelle*. She was coming back from a three day lining trip one hundred miles offshore and she looked really fine with her large brown sail billowing out over the bow. I asked Jimmy Madron in the Ship Inn one evening if the foresail made any difference to their time. He was the skipper of the *Renovelle*. He said that with a following wind and a fair breeze it saved an hour on a one hundred mile trip, so they would save an hours worth of fuel as well. Long lining died out in the early 1970's mainly due to the high cost of bait, now there are only a few inshore boats that occasionally work a thousand hook line but even this has basically died out because the price of Conger Eels has dropped so dramatically. But like other types of fish the price will increase at some stage and then small inshore vessels will take up this type of fishing again. I don't think the big long line fishing boats will ever make a comeback. They used to shoot thousands of hooks up to one hundred miles offshore. Crabbers occasionally catch Congers in their pots which are either released or cut up for crab-pot bait. I would say that anglers fishing on wrecks or high reefs take more Conger in a year than commercial boats. The biggest Conger I caught weighed one hundred and nine pounds after being gutted. This fine eel was caught on a long line that I shot alongside the *City of Westminster* wreck at the Runnel Stone. Anglers fishing deep water wrecks have taken even larger Conger on rod and reel. The *Fishing News* for commercial fishing vessels reported that a long liner fishing for Tuna and Swordfish in the Azores had caught a Conger that weighed nine hundred pounds - so how big they *can* grow has never really been established. I can't remember the date but think it was in the 1960's or 70's. After the Second World War the Mediterranean Sea was full of wartime wrecks that blocked harbours and harbour approaches. When these wrecks were blown up there were numerous reports from divers of Conger weighing two or three hundred pounds being killed. In 2012 there was a documentary on television showing North Sea divers inspecting oil platforms and pipes. Every so often the cameraman would pan out to show a very large fish alongside the diver. There was one Cod that was much larger than the diver and would probably have a mouth big enough to fit the diver inside. Another shot was taken of two pipes, as the camera panned out the largest pipe turned out to be a massive Conger resting against the smaller pipe. No commercial or pleasure vessels are allowed to fish anywhere near these oil rigs or pipelines for obvious reasons and so the fish can grow very large in a safe environment.

One of the most frequent accidents involving commercial fishing and pleasure boats including yachts occurs during poor visibility, rain, hail, snow or fog and happens every year around our coasts. A large oil tanker or container ship can cut a boat in half and not even know they have hit anything. Most times there is nothing to show where she sank, not even the salt water activated distress beacon survives the impact and it can be days or even weeks before the wreck is found - a few times it is never discovered. Once found the Marine Safety Inspection team usually send down a remote controlled camera first to inspect the wreck. This normally gives some indication of why she sank. If it was a collision then paint samples are taken and these are passed to the Harbourmasters of every port around the world to check each tanker or container ship for a match. In a very few cases they are lucky and the skipper gets prosecuted but in the vast majority of cases nothing is ever found and that vessel and skipper never realise that they have sunk another boat. But that is just another one of the hazards you face when you put to sea for pleasure or a living in a small boat.

It is not only boats, coastlines or harbours that get damaged during a southerly storm but cars as well. How many cars have been damaged or written off over the years that have been parked on Mousehole's quays is not known but it must be at least one hundred. The huge waves sweeping the quays can just crumple a car up pushing the roof down to the car floor. Others are washed under the railings and get jammed solid. Some get filled up with sand and shingle where roofs or windows have been stoved in. A few are lucky and driven off but all will be affected by the sea water and rust out quickly. The majority are usually scrapped because it would cost the insurance companies too much money to replace all the electrics. This happened to three brand new cars on the Old Quay. The owners were trying to sell them in the pub for £10 – a new BMW and two new Volvos – there were no takers. They were towed away to the scrapyard – their insides full of sand and sea water.

The photographs shown in this book are wrecks that have happened over the years near Mousehole. I have only included one or two photographs from each of the series I took at the time. I was the only person to get pictures of some wrecks because I was in the L.S.A. The *Torrey Canyon* photos I got from a Culdrose pilot who was selling them in all the local pubs at 2/6d for five photographs. The *Golden Corn* wreck was the same day I had to have my dog put down through old age.